No More
Dancing Chickens!

Empowering Families to Stay Connected in a Disconnected World

Phillip M. Taylor

5 Fold Media
Visit us at www.5foldmedia.com

No More Dancing Chickens!: Empowering Families to Stay Connected in a Disconnected World
Copyright 2014 by Phillip Taylor
Published by 5 Fold Media, LLC
www.5foldmedia.com

ISBN: 978-1-936578-99-3
Library of Congress Control Number: 2014944989

I want to dedicate this book to my dear friend, Joel Hedlund, whose endorsement of this book came only months before being diagnosed with a glioblastoma tumor of the brain. The unwavering faith and joy he has demonstrated in the grueling presence of cancer has inspired the lives of so many, including my own. You represent Jesus so well!

I also want to dedicate this book to the people who, after reading it, will choose to no longer live life as a dancing chicken.

Acknowledgments

No book is written without the significant contributions and loving support of caring and gifted people. I want to give special heartfelt thanks to the following people for helping make this book possible:

- My amazing wife, Shannon, for her constant belief in me as a person and as a writer.

- My children, Mallorie, Bradley, and Kelly, for loving me in spite of my many parenting failures and for teaching me so much about life.

- My always supportive mom and dad, Glenn and Jo Ann Taylor; my brother, Stewert, and his family; my amazing in-laws, Jimmy and Becky Bradley, who entrusted to me the hand of their firstborn daughter; and all of my extended family.

- Andy and Trisha O'Neil, for their faithful friendship and relentless efforts of cleaning up my writing messes and encouraging me to never stop writing.

- Andy and Cathy Sanders, along with the incredible team at 5 Fold Media for helping make this dream a reality.

Endorsements

"Phillip Taylor provides practical help for anyone with an out-of-control life. If you're tired and weary of the cultural 'chicken dance,' this book will encourage you with wisdom and insights for life at its best!"

Rick Whitmer
Senior Director, Ron Hutchcraft Ministries
Harrison, Arkansas

"As a busy mom of two young children, there are a few things I look for in a book. I need something that is easy to read, with practical advice that gives me something 'deep' to think on through the day, written by an author who is transparent and honest. This book delivered on all accounts. Mr. Taylor depicts parenting, marriage, and all relationships in light of everyday struggles, hurts, failures, and successes. This is a must read for anyone that has any contact with people!"

Lori Holbert
West Virginia

"I have had the privilege of knowing Phillip for nearly thirty years. What gives this book the most weight and impact is the fact that I have seen him live this and have observed him grow immensely as a friend, husband, father, and a Christian leader. Reading this came at a pretty ironic time in my life while I was stepping out of the limelight to invest in my family. It has already helped put some framework to my new way of living. I found his words to be very insightful as well as practical; the follow-up sections at the end of each chapter are challenging and prompt you to action, rather than leaving you with mere inspiration."

Joel Hedlund, videographer
Hawaii

"I felt like Mr. Taylor's book was speaking directly to me while reading it. My family is going through things mentioned in this book and I appreciated the clarity and honesty in which the book was written."

Melissa Stimson
Elementary School Teacher
Green Forest, Arkansas

Contents

Foreword

It is an honor for me to introduce Phillip Taylor and his insightful book on life, *No More Dancing Chickens!* I have known Phillip for several years and have served on staff with him in two different ministries. However, I really got to know him during a trip to a church conference in Dallas. After the event, we forfeited another night's hotel stay and decided to "cowboy up" and drive all night. Phillip and I made lifelong memories on that journey as we shared personal stories and lots of laughter about our lives and all the messiness of ministry.

Speaking of messy, I will never forget—with each pit stop Phillip's normally-groomed hair became increasingly out of place (seeming to stick two feet up in the air) as he had rubbed his face and run his hands through his hair. It is in the weary moments like this when you truly fellowship and personally connect with someone during the long voyages of life.

Every person has probably rubbed their hands through their hair in despair when trying to relate to someone. Phillip's genuine people skills and passion will comb through the tangles in your relationships. He expresses himself in a refreshingly simple and practical manner, empowering you to straighten out the relational messes in your life. Instead of saying that Phillip "lets his hair down," let's say he "lets his hair up" in this writing to reveal his "messed up" experiences that God has moved him to communicate in this powerful message.

Pastor Heath Kirkpatrick
Woodland Heights Baptist Church
Harrison, Arkansas

Introduction: Houston, We Have a Problem

I have a great sense of obligation to people in both the civilized world and the rest of the world" (Romans 1:14). These words were penned around 2,000 years ago by a man named Paul in a letter to people of the Christian faith in Rome as he described his life's calling to make a lasting imprint on the world around him.

I guess you could say I also share a great sense of obligation to our culture. It is an obligation and passion to see people restored to a place of true connection with those they love the most, in ways that last longer than a text message or social media post. It is a passion to provide an alternate route to daily living that keeps us from being taken over by our culture's unrealistic demands and expectations. Why should this matter to us? In the famous words spoken by John Swigert, Jr. during the US Apollo 13 moon flight, "Houston, we've had a problem here."

The Battle We Are Losing

A problem we have had indeed. The problem for many of us is that our lives feel out of control. We are tired. We are bound under layers of stress that keep us from truly living life. It is not that we can get by in life without working hard. It is the fact that we have become so defined by what we do that we have lost sight of what really is supposed to matter. We are so busy making a living that we forget to make a life. The culture in which we live has done a good job convincing us that this is normal. By culture, I am referring to a mindset that busy is always

13

better. It can come from individuals or groups alike. Regardless of the source, their pressure is felt and must be recognized as a major culprit, influencing our driven lifestyles, devoid of rest.

Many would never admit it, but deep down they have given up hope of life being something they could ever really enjoy. We simply get out of bed every morning and endure whatever comes our way. Even when things seem to go well, we hold our breath, waiting in anticipation for the other shoe to fall. With this as our mindset, we are left with only a distant dream of maybe one day catching a break, of one day getting our joy back, of one day getting our heart back and actually looking forward to what the next day holds.

> Many would never admit it, but deep down we have given up hope of life being at all enjoyable.

Our lives can also be described as ships at sea with no definite course. We are constantly, aggressively overexposed to every wind of cultural influence that blows through, telling us loudly how successful people dress, act, smell, drive, raise kids, experience romance, work, vacation, and retire. After all, the "American Dream" is about measurable success, right?

When stress and fatigue are combined with relentless cultural pressures to keep up with the Joneses, relationships inevitably come in at a distant second to our own survival. Living free is nowhere on the radar, and truly nurturing our closest relationships becomes a mere afterthought. The result is a deafening disconnection with those we love and care about the most. Even though we live in the most technological age known to man with the ability to communicate with someone around the world in a matter of seconds, we have become the most disconnected generation of all time.

Think about it. When is the last time you had an enjoyable, face-to-face conversation with someone you are close to? Let us take it a step further. Who would even make your list of people you consider yourself close to? My guess is the list is very short if it exists at all.

In a hard-driving culture, with very few stop signs, we stand at a crossroads that demands we look life in the eye and examine where it is leading us. An honest assessment of where we are headed will expose the undeniable, stark-naked truth that we stand in need of change. We are desperate for a different road upon which to travel. Without it, we will only continue to find ourselves existing on the path that promises an illusion of success and happiness. While we watch the things we truly value—our relationships—continue to disappear like a mist in the fog, we spend the rest of our time covering ourselves with fig leaves, hoping we aren't exposed as the empty, hurting, and confused people we really are.

Does such a different road, one of lasting hope and true connection with those closest to you, exist? Or is it something of the past? Is it possible for your family to live deeply connected to one another and still fulfill their responsibilities and purpose? If so, how do you even begin taking steps toward this without completely derailing the train of daily living and schedules? It is my desire in this book to provide an alternate route for you to consider—no matter where you are in your journey.

This is not about another money making strategy that promises to change your economic status significantly within six months so that you can spend more time at home. Perhaps most importantly, this is also not intended to be a success story of how I used to be where you are and, with a huge break that came my way, managed to conquer everything holding me back in life so that I no longer have worries or problems.

Quite the opposite is true. I am a working man living in the thick of life as a school teacher and coach, as a husband and a father. My wife also works out of the home and makes countless sacrifices so that we can make ends meet. We are raising two children. I know the heartache of broken dreams and the many unexpected turns life can take without advanced notice. I share these vulnerable snapshots so that you will know I am a real person, facing real challenges.

15

However, the painful struggles I have endured that have brought me to where I am today—which I will share in later chapters—have caused me to look at life much differently than in times past. They have motivated me to examine my truest values. In the process, the fog has cleared from my vision of where I want to go as an individual and where I want to lead my family.

There is a new road upon which I want to travel. It is a road that has given me new life, brought my family closer than ever before, and is paving the way to a hope-filled future. I want to share it with you.

My motivation for writing this book has not only come from my own personal story, but also from the countless stories of families with whom I have had the privilege of working in the context of local churches, the mental health world, and the public school system. Here is the bottom-line truth that has anchored this work: people are hurting and families are more spread out and stretched thinner than ever before. It is for the cause of families that this book has been written.

I want to inspire and motivate change in the lives of people who are tired of living life according to what the culture says is the way to go in order to be successful. In all of our culture's attempts to drive us toward success, we still have an overwhelming percentage of family breakups, resulting in a multitude of younger generations being left with some pretty tough questions to try to answer about how life is really supposed to work. The future is at stake for families, and it is time that we recognize that what we are doing simply is not working. We must have a change in how we approach life. While this book is no fix-all approach, its purpose is deeply ingrained in a desire to make a lasting difference for as many as possible while there is still time.

This is why I want to invite and empower you, beginning today, to identify and live out your true values and priorities, rather than trying to merely adjust your current economic status in an effort to find more happiness or trying to make a balanced life your ultimate goal. I want you to not only survive in this breakneck pace of a culture we find ourselves in, but to thrive. To really live. To smile and mean it. To allow the colorless, bland monotony of your daily life to once again be filled with vibrant colors of purpose and meaning. I believe such a road exists, and I am one who is pursuing it with passion. There is no greater time than now to begin, and now is all we are guaranteed.

> An honest assessment of where we are headed will expose the undeniable, stark-naked truth that we stand in need of change.

One more thing I want you to know is that I fail regularly at following my own advice. Any direction and insights given in this book are not from an expert's point of view, but rather from a deeply flawed man trying to work his way through what it means to raise a family and make the most out of life. I am coming to you as a learner. Yet I hope in some way that something that is said can be beneficial to you as we walk together in this journey of understanding more of what it means to live connected lives with those closest to us.

As you make your way through this book, I encourage you to reflect on the motivating questions found in the "Making It Personal" sections that close each chapter. These are designed to help you apply what you have read and develop your own strategy of learning how to become more and more the family and the individual you were meant to be. To begin, you need to understand and embrace "The Power of Permission."

Chapter 1

The Power of
Permission

Chapter 1: The Power of Permission

"The thief's purpose is to steal and kill and destroy.
My purpose is to give them a rich and satisfying life"
(John 10:10).

Most of us have heard stories about dancing chickens. Somewhere along the way, the idea surfaced of placing a live chicken on a stage to perform for a crowd. By placing a heating element under the stage and gradually turning up the heat, the chicken ideally would hop back and forth on the stage as if it were dancing. Quite a sideshow, for sure, if you could get the act to work properly!

The chicken is not likely to recognize the gradual increase of the heat on the stage until it becomes uncomfortably hot enough that its natural reaction is to start hopping around. This scenario begs the question: what keeps the chicken from jumping off the stage? Perhaps it becomes disoriented and confused about its surroundings, or maybe it does not realize it has the permission to jump off. Whatever the case, this type of act soon became a main attraction at places like county fairs. Everyone wanted to see the dancing chicken.

Like the chicken, many of us have become immune to the gradual increase of pressure and unhealthy expectations being placed upon us by today's culture. The results, by and large, are many good families hopping around on the world's stage, attempting to perform for an audience that really could care less about their well-being. In the meantime, they have lost sight of the fact that there is another option available: hopping off the stage and no longer choosing to perform for people who really do not add anything to their lives.

I myself have experienced times of living like a dancing chicken much of my adult life. Often without realizing it, I have allowed myself to be dictated by others' unrealistic expectations of me instead of living my life from my heart, from a true center. Unfortunately, the consequences of this mindset have not ended with me. I eventually ended up leading my family down a similar path. It was not until a couple of years ago that my eyes began to open to the truth of what had been happening to us.

My family, for the most part, was being dragged through life by many different voices and influences; most were very well-meaning, I might add. It was as if we were in the middle of a river, trying our best to reach down and plant our feet firmly on the bottom to gain a sense of stability and identity, only to be swept away by the fast-moving and overwhelming current of everyone else's expectations. We simply could not keep up.

At some point, I remember waking up one day and embracing the fact that I was tired, my family was worn out from living like this, and something had to change. I was not quite sure what it was exactly that I needed to change or how to go about it, but one thing was sure: I was tired of living my life as a dancing chicken.

Perhaps it is because you feel this way that you chose to pick up and read this book. Perhaps you have allowed yourself and even your family to get so caught up in trying to meet the many expectations and demands of the people around you (all the while doing some really good things) that you have completely lost connection with each other. You have lost heart and lost any real direction for where you want to go. Perhaps you are recognizing that your family is strung out, going through the motions, and it is time to bring significant change before it is too late.

If this is the case, or anything similar to it, I welcome you to the starting line of a brand new adventure. I can tell you that the road ahead is not one of ease and comfort but one of struggle if you really intend to change the way you live. It will be a journey of conflict and one of constant re-adjustment to everything to which you are accustomed. But the rewards will be worth any price you have to pay if it means getting you and your family back on track and choosing to no longer live like dancing chickens.

Preparing for Battle

One of the first reality checks you will face when making strides toward changing how you approach life will be that change brings conflict. I wish I could say it in a more palatable way, but there really is no way around it. If you want to hop off the stage and no longer perform for the applause of the world, you can expect that not everyone will be in agreement with your decisions, including some of the people who are closest to you. In fact, they very well may turn on you like sharks in bloody water.

Not only will you face opposition from others, but you will also have to face conflict within yourself. Your old way of doings things will never look and feel more appealing than when you begin taking steps in the opposite direction of what you are used to doing in your daily life and decision-making. It will be difficult to confront your own personal feelings of having lived under the thumb of someone's (or something's) control that has been keeping you from being your best. I have had to do this many, many times and in many different contexts. Each time I have been faced with this type of uncomfortable decision-making, something inside of me tried to minimize its effects on me so that I would not have to confront people or harmful circumstances. I just wanted it to go away.

As I have grown, however, my heart has not allowed me to sweep things like this under the rug anymore. I am learning to deal honestly with what is going on inside of me—for my sake and for the sake of others— instead of stuffing it and going about my business. For some of you, the idea that these things are an issue may seem ridiculous. For others, this is speaking to something deep within you that you need to hear.

> There is nothing like knowing you have done everything in your power to live at peace with yourself and to live in truth with others.

I am thankful for each time that I do the right thing by appropriately confronting the all-consuming expectations and demands that squelch my potential or hurt my relationships with others. While there must be good use of discernment with each situation to know how to respond, the payoff is immeasurable when you can lay your head on your pillow at night with a clear heart, knowing you have done everything in your power to live at peace with yourself and to live in truth with others. The alternative of bottling up your emotions and dying from the inside out under the weight of unhealthy expectations just is not a viable option anymore. It is time to hop off the stage and no longer be okay with living as a dancing chicken.

Let us turn the tables and put the ball in your court. My desire is to help you move confidently into the potentially deep waters that tend to surround the idea of confronting hurtful expectations that have held you captive for far too long. For you to move in that direction effectively, we need to spend some time clarifying expectations for where we want to go and what we want to avoid.

A Word about Expectations

Allow me to be clear on what I am advocating regarding the situations or people we may need to confront who seem to keep you dancing on that stage. I am referring to unhealthy, controlling, and oftentimes debilitating expectations that negatively affect your well-being and the health of your closest relationships. These types of expectations stifle your strongest gifts and abilities, keeping you sidetracked from reaching your potential. These types of expectations can come from the culture in general or from specific individuals.

It would be easy for you to rationalize a choice to leave your spouse or quit your job in an attempt to get out from under someone's expectations or to "find the real you." While a job change may eventually become necessary, this is not about permission to walk away from your daily responsibilities and commitments. There are plenty of people in the world who are doing that and to increase their number would only serve to make matters worse.

We are not attempting to throw the baby out with the bathwater. Life is full of healthy and necessary expectations that keep the world turning. When I go to a restaurant, I expect timely service and quality food. Your boss has very necessary expectations that you will be at work on time every day, fulfill your job duties excellently, and that you will not make excuses for why you cannot get a job completed. Life is also hard, and you may be under an employer whose demands push you to the limit, and occasionally beyond, when they see greater potential in you. These are not things I am addressing as unrealistic expectations.

Having said that, I now want you to pause long enough to spend some time identifying unhealthy expectations you are striving to meet and the people you are unrealistically trying to please in your daily life. You might be surprised at what emotions come to the surface and whose faces suddenly appear as you give this considerable thought. Is the nagging voice from the perfectionist parent of your childhood still communicating that nothing you do is ever good enough? Is it the in-laws who are waiting for you to fail, while claiming to always know what is best? Is it a certain pressure coming from your friends? Your pastor? Your church?

The list could include many or few whose unrealistic or hurtful expectations are having a significant impact on you. While many expectations from others simply need to be ignored, other sources of expectations can take a real toll on you. What is important is that you listen to yourself and be honest. Who is *really* calling the shots in your life?

The Root of the Issue

Chances are, if you struggle with trying to meet everyone's expectations, it may be because you have lived with an overwhelming fear of letting people down. If this is the case with you, I can very much relate to that as a part of my journey. While there is no doubt that we feel valued when people give us an "A" on our life's report card, the constant search for approval or validation from others can also become an addiction that fuels your every decision, because the thought of not having someone's approval can feel like death. Like an alcoholic who constantly thirsts for one more drink, validation addicts find themselves searching for one more "Atta boy!" from people who are supposed to matter.

Ultimately, this kind of fear comes from believing the lie that without the right person's approval, your life loses value. Suffice it to say that even as I write this book, I am faced with the challenge of wanting my efforts to be noticed and to be seen as valuable by certain people. None of us are immune.

> It is time to release yourself from trying to be someone you are not, just to try to please someone else.

For all of us, though, the time has come. It is time to give ourselves permission to no longer need the applause of those people who have served tirelessly as the self-appointed committee on our decisions. It is time to make some very necessary changes in how you approach life. If you do not, you may risk losing your heart forever.

Maybe you have lived for so long under the thumb of certain people or circumstances that you have lost any sense of living from a true center, from being your true self. If that is the case, you definitely need to draw for yourself a new starting line. You need to discover who you are and who you were really meant to be. It is time to release yourself from trying to be someone you are not, just to try to please someone else. Give yourself permission to take your life back and start living again. Your closest relationships, as we will see, are depending on it.

Take time to think. Reflect. Allow yourself to feel, realizing what is at stake if your current path of living and decision-making results in anything other than a strong connection to those closest to you and the fulfillment of heartfelt purpose. It is time to take back the ground that is rightfully yours. Your life is too valuable to continue living it as a dancing chicken.

As you begin taking steps toward confronting the harmful expectations that have held you down for so long and you open yourself up to this new way of living life for the right reasons, you will soon discover how much you have missed by not being the real you. There is no overnight fix for your life. The more time you give this process, however, the less glamorous your old way of living life will become. You will soon realize that the pursuit of the American Dream as you have known it, along with its unruly expectations, has taken the very life out of you that it promised to provide.

You will also discover that the people who have held you captive through unhealthy expectations really contribute very little to your life. Most of all, you will be in a place to realize "The Power of Priorities."

> Your life is too valuable to continue living it as a dancing chicken.

Making It Personal

- Now that you've read this chapter on "The Power of Permission," who are the people serving faithfully as the self-appointed committee on your decisions? How have they affected you?

- Up to this point in your journey, how well have you handled conflict with others? What thought, idea, or emotion comes over you when considering the need to confront certain people for the ways they have hurt you or held you back from your potential with harmful or unrealistic expectations?

- Do you have a time frame in mind for beginning to deal with these harmful expectations from others? What first step will you need to take?

Chapter 2

The Power of Priorities

Chapter 2: The Power of Priorities

"Your own ears will hear him. Right behind you a voice will say, 'This is the way you should go,' whether to the right or to the left" (Isaiah 30:21).

Until two years ago or so, my family led a fast and furious lifestyle. Like many families striving to make life work while hoping to make a lasting difference with those they influence, we had been known for saying no to very few things, and yes to everything we thought we could and should be doing. After all, unless you are a cat with nine lives, you can only live life once! In truth, my wife and I were over-involved in the community, and our children were reaching ages of being involved more and more in activities outside of the home too. We were literally meeting ourselves coming and going. You know the feeling. You have been there, and you may be there still.

Looking back, you could have easily described my family as adrenaline junkies, but of a different sort. We weren't jumping off tall cliffs (I hate heights) or seeing how large of an explosion we could legally create in our backyard. Instead, we were living off the adrenaline that you get when your personal sense of value gets wrapped up in your performance. If we were not busy doing something, we felt as if we were failing—failing our kids, our friends, our church, and each other. After all, who gets applause for taking a needed nap? As time would tell, this lifestyle would soon change, but in a manner least expected and least desired.

The Alarm Clocks of Life

When I was a child, I had the most annoying alarm clock known to man. It was a bell alarm clock that sounded like an emergency alert at a local fire station when it went off. It would scare you very much awake! I hated the thing. Little did I know that it was only a humorous precursor to the ways life would abruptly wake me up at different times and in different seasons with crises of all shapes and sizes. My family likely would have remained on the blazing path of busyness in pursuit of the American dream we had so firmly established in our minds had it not been for some key crisis moments that made their appearance without an invitation. These crises were loud enough to catch our attention and cause us to evaluate how reckless our existing path of living was that we were so faithfully following.

Typically, when crises come, they hit you in one of three areas and can often involve a strange combination of all three—financially, physically, and relationally. Do any of these sound familiar to you? During this season of our lives, we were hit hard in all three.

> Typically, when crises come, they hit you in one of three areas and can often involve a strange combination of all three—financially, physically, and relationally.

Financially

For starters, I went one year and two months without a salary. I let go of a very stable job with good benefits to pursue an exciting job opportunity somewhere else that seemed promising at the time. After several months of giving it the old college try, it became clear that the opportunity was not going to develop into what we thought it would be. It was like the release of one trapeze, only to discover that the next trapeze was not anywhere in sight. I was not without work, but the idea of me being the primary breadwinner of our home was suddenly out of reach. No matter how diligently I applied for good paying jobs and no matter how many side jobs I could come up with to help bridge the gap, I was not even coming close. As a husband and father, this was a huge stress contributor in my life, to say the least. Over time, not being able to provide for my home resulted in feelings of depression and an overwhelming sense of inadequacy and failure. If you really want to test a man, take away his ability to provide sufficiently for his home and see what happens. Though I have been blessed to have secured a steady job since then, and though God provided many different temporary safety nets along the way, we still feel the effects of that hard season of going without my consistent income, and we will for some time.

Physically

What followed on the heels of that season without adequate income was another financial challenge, combined with a merciless breakdown in my wife's health. Due to a recurring back injury, my wife was forced to relinquish much of her work as a speech therapist. Having suffered a herniated disk in her lower back (L4-L5) nine years ago, she has had her ups and downs dealing with the injury. Until a year or so ago, the injury was mostly manageable by being aware of her movements and not overdoing it on physical activity. A tough challenge for any active mom!

However, what we were not prepared for was the way stress from the previous years of our daily pace of living (and my loss of income) would eventually catch up with her. It was as if the stress she absorbed in her body all settled in the exact location of her lower back where the injury occurred. As the months passed, she regressed from a relatively normal, active lifestyle of working five days a week to being unable to accomplish even the most menial tasks at home or elsewhere. She became unable to enjoy a night out with her girlfriends or even sit up for any lengthy period of time just to watch television without severe and debilitating pain.

For roughly six weeks, the protocol for her life was to stay in bed or on the couch and let her body rest. The pain had grown to become so unbearable at times that she was unable to get up from a lying position for any reason other than to use the restroom. The thought of attempting to go anywhere on her own was out of the question. Want to take a walk with the kids on a sunny day? Sorry, no can do. Want to hop in the car and drive forty-five minutes to spend time at a cookout with relatives? Nice idea, thanks for playing. At the end of the six weeks of lying on her back, her body slowly started giving her some relief. She was able to get out of bed on her own, walk around the house, and even begin taking the kids to school again on certain days when she felt up to it. If you have suffered a severe back injury, you can definitely relate to what she went through.

We have since been able to provide her with what we believe to be effective medical help and are confident she is on her road to healing. She has been able to return to work a few days a week for up to three or four hours at a time. However, it goes without saying that the physical, emotional, and financial windstorm that accompanied her loss of health, combined with both of us losing substantial incomes over the course of roughly two years, left their imprint.

Relationally

If you asked me today what has changed the most in our day-to-day lives, I would give you a one-word response— priorities.

At the helm of these crises came yet another painful transition. This time it was that of leaving a local faith community into which we had invested five years of our lives and which had invested richly into us. For our family, the local church is vital to our home life, and it has been where our closest relationships have developed. We could not have imagined this shift in our hearts taking place that would bring us to the decision of leaving this local body of believers at such a crucial point in our lives, but we knew deep down this was the direction we were being called to go.

If you have ever had the experience of leaving a local church, whether for good or for bad, it does not take a lot of convincing to recognize that it can be an extremely painful process. For six to eight months, we sensed through a number of factors that we would eventually be uprooted and led to serve God in a different capacity and in a different place, though we did not know where or how. While we were very thankful for the many ways this great church invested in us as a family, the time came for us to step away. As part of this decision, many relationships ended up being strained, and some were even lost in the maze of misunderstandings. It was unavoidable. Needless to say, the weight of this transition just added to the mix of everything else we were still reeling from physically and financially.

Undoubtedly, there will be many reading this who have undergone trials and hardships much more severe than what I have described as part of our story. The point I want to make is that the cumulative effect of all this on us was motivation enough to want to change how we lived. This helped me remember that pain is never wasted if we learn something from it.

My father has told me more than once that he believes the greatest motivation for change is pain. Little did we know how much our lives would be changed from these previous twenty-four months of challenges we endured. If you asked me today what has changed the most in our day-to-day lives, I would give you a one-word response—priorities.

No More Lip Service

It is amazing how we give lip service to many priorities without really demonstrating any kind of commitment to those priorities. Even the items on our priority list that we give time and attention to can be easily compromised if we can get by with doing less and if what little we do seems to be working.

For instance, unless a husband and wife outright hate one another they would likely claim that their marriage is at the top of the of priorities. "My family is all that matters to me!" th

Most married couples would agree. However, through some basic investigating into the relationship, it may be easier to conclude that the marriage is really not a couple's highest priority. The marriage may just happen to not be falling apart. For all we know, they may have a list a mile long for why they are choosing to avoid any meaningful conversations with one another. They may be completely at odds about how to raise the kids or manage the budget. As long as they perceive the marriage to be doing okay the way things are (i.e., as long as no one has threatened to walk out), they will continue holding to the claim that their marriage is a high priority.

Through the many challenges I have described, I can safely say that my wife and I have experienced an authentic shift in priorities, beginning in our marriage. While we had a very solid marriage prior to the events mentioned, the pain we have gone through has served to make us stronger and bring us closer together than ever before. Along with this new closeness have come important decisions, which I hope will remain as anchors that keep us from going adrift in the years to come. One such decision involves putting our marriage first above anything else. The second is securing direction for our family above any other social expectation or agenda. Both are easier said than done, but are absolutely essential to keeping us off the stage as dancing chickens.

Putting Your Marriage First

The difference between saying that your marriage is your top priority and your marriage actually being your top priority is the action you take based on that conviction. For us, everything we have walked through together in the last twenty years of being together has led us to not only solidify the priority of our marriage, but to also wrap a banner of support around our marriage to keep it our first priority. The banner looks like this: We plan everything around our marriage. Before making significant decisions that affect our home, we are learning to ask this one question: How will this affect our marriage? This includes job choices, vacations, friendship choices, and the like.

36

> The difference between saying that your marriage is your top priority and your marriage actually being your top priority is the action you take based on that conviction.

To help us simplify the answer to the question of how certain things may affect our marriage, we have had to change our basic formula for how we approach life. When we were single and satisfied, and even into the first several years of our marriage, our decision-making formula looked like this:

I can = I will.

> No harm, no foul. If I wanted to do something, I did it. The same went with her. Nearly two decades later, however, our formula has changed to reflect one of the following two outcomes, depending on the circumstances: If the timing is right and we both feel good about it, the formula looks like this:

I can + we can = I will.

> Consequently, if the timing is not right or we both do not feel good about a decision, it looks something like this:

I can + we cannot = I will wait.

In other words, we are learning how much one's decisions affect the other and vice versa. There have been a number of things I have wanted to do out of pure personal enjoyment and desire for adventure that my wife has fully supported. Writing this book is one of them. There have also been some great and exciting things she or I have wanted to pursue that would have had the potential to negatively impact our marriage to which we have had to say no. The difference is not the quality of the opportunities. The issue is a sensitivity to one another that allows us to say *yes* to the right things and *no* or *not now* to the things that fall in inappropriate timing or do not support our family's vision.

The idea of scheduling everything around our marriage has become a lifesaver for us. Just by making that one decision alone, a ton of other decisions are already made without having to worry about them. This concept of the marriage being central is not confined to marriage retreat weekends with our church or an occasional date night; it applies to all of our decisions throughout the year. If we are exhausted one evening and need to catch up on one another's lives, we may skip out on attending one of our kid's athletic events so that we can have time together. If our plate of responsibilities is causing us to live and lead from exhaustion instead of out of rest, leaving us with nothing left to give our family, we back down a bit and eliminate things that are not live-or-die time consumers. You get the picture. You will never regret prioritizing your marriage and securing it with a commitment to keep it fresh and enjoyable.

To take this idea further of making your marriage your top priority, I am honored to draw thoughts from my father, Dr. Glenn Taylor, who has been married to my mom now for fifty-two years and has served his community as a licensed counselor for twenty-eight years. He has provided a short set of simple and penetrating questions followed by brief descriptions that can help you identify areas of needed change in your life, which can have a significant effect on your marriage relationship.

He says, "These four questions, if answered correctly, can totally revolutionize your marriage."

1. Am I easy to live with, or is it my way or the highway? Do I have to be right? Am I someone my spouse looks forward to coming home to at day's end, or is that something they dread?

2. Am I easy to love? Am I tender and affectionate, or distant and cold?

3. Am I easy to talk to, or am I defensive, argumentative, harsh, angry, and critical?

4. Am I fun to be with? Do I like to do fun things? Do I laugh a lot? Do I know how to lighten up and enjoy life? Do I bring smiles to those around me and add to their joy?

He concludes, "How do you know if the answer to these questions is yes or no? You can ask yourself these questions, but you are not likely to be honest. You can ask God, but it is doubtful you will listen to His response. Lastly and what is most recommended, you can ask your spouse! They will be the most honest with you and will be more likely to work alongside you to reach great results in your marriage relationship."

> You will never regret prioritizing your marriage and securing it with a commitment to keep it fresh and enjoyable.

Securing Your Family

The second decision coming from the shift in our priorities is the idea of scheduling everything else around our family. Not to be confused with the first priority of building life around your marriage, this priority extends to the needs of your children. If we are being honest, this is where the cultural pressures are really felt if you dare to not live like a dancing chicken.

Let me ask you an honest question. How hard is it for you to say *no* to things your kids want to do? Better yet, how hard is it for you to say *no* to things that other people want your kids to do? For my family, it is a case by case basis. We want our kids to hear *yes* from us more than they hear *no*, and we want them to have as many great life experiences as possible. However, our new set of priorities leads us to look at things through a broader lens. At the end of the day, there are some opportunities for our kids that do not necessarily fall into the categories of right or wrong, safe or unsafe. Rather, the question should be, "Is this option the best option for us *as a family* right now?" As a very simple example, instead of the kids going to a friend's house for a sleepover at the end of a tiring week, being home together around an evening a meal and sleeping in on Saturday morning may be the better option before the start of yet another week.

I recently asked my wife and kids to stay home from church on a Sunday morning while I went ahead and attended. My family was worn out from many consecutive days and evenings of schoolwork, tests, ballgames, and the like. They needed to rest more than they needed to be at church. As a pastoral leader in our church, some may consider my decision to be hypocritical. I say it is the most honorable decision I could have made on behalf of my family. To borrow from chapter one, you must decide who is calling the shots in your life. Then plan accordingly. I am very blessed to have a pastor who is gracious and understanding and who is leading the charge in desiring what is best for the family above anything else that may be going on at the church.

Your situation may be a little different, and you may have to be more creative in fighting for the well-being of your home, depending on the circumstances. The key is keeping your thumb on the pulse of your family while taking care of the things that need to be done. If things get out of whack at home, they will eventually affect your performance at work and elsewhere.

Recognize Your Capacity

Not every family operates the same, nor does every marriage. Your marriage has a different capacity for activity and being on the go than my family. The important action or step you need to take is to determine what that capacity is for you as a couple, for your spouse as an individual, for your children, and for you personally. As you identify everyone's capacities, you can then make much better decisions that benefit everyone in your household. In turn, you will eliminate a lot of unnecessary stress felt by one or more family members who may not be able to keep up with your ideal pace of living and accomplishing tasks. To bring the idea of priorities into greater light, let's do a case study.

Brian and Jennifer (fictitious names) have been married for twelve years and have three children—a daughter, age ten; a son, age eight; and a youngest daughter, age four. Brian is a very outgoing and influential businessman. He travels one hundred and fifty days a year. He is involved in a number of civic groups, contributes to a few highly effective charities, and enjoys being part of a local hunting club on most weekends in the fall and spring. Brian is also a recovering alcoholic. As a result, his deepest passion in life is helping men in the community overcome their alcohol (and other related) addictions. He meets with a group of these men for two hours on Thursday nights when he is in town.

Jennifer is an online sales rep for a nationally known retail company, which allows her to work at home. She stays busy with a thirty-five to forty hour work week in addition to keeping a watchful eye on their youngest daughter, who is in preschool for two half days each week. Jennifer takes all three kids to school and picks them up. Her favorite hobby is joining in with a few girlfriends every other Tuesday night for dinner and a fun leisure game. She would tell you she loves her husband, and her greatest passion is being able to be there for her children's activities, which continue to increase as they get older.

Just last fall, Jennifer's oldest daughter decided she wanted to try taking voice lessons on Monday evenings, in addition to violin lessons on Thursdays right after school and being on the gymnastics travel squad almost every weekend. Her son plays pee wee basketball every Saturday morning for eight weeks in the fall, baseball for eight weeks in the spring, and also recently decided he wants to take private guitar lessons.

Jennifer has begun to feel not only the weight of her successful, increasingly demanding job, but also the weight of taking care of the daily needs of her family in Brian's absence. Brian, however, does not see how his absence from home is affecting Jennifer, and is, in fact, ready to start a second men's group which would meet on the Sunday nights he is in town, after hearing that other men wanted to get involved. After all, Brian's heart really goes out to these men and wants to see them succeed by moving past their addictions. To Brian, his job is just a way to make money, but the men in these addiction groups really stir the passion inside of him to make a difference.

One more dynamic is about to enter the picture for Jennifer and Brian. Brian's sister is going through an ugly divorce and has asked Brian if he would consider allowing her two daughters, aged 13 and 11, to come and live with them on alternate weekends until things get settled down. Brian has not said anything about this to Jennifer, but he feels sure she will understand and want to help his sister's family.

As you can tell from this all-too-common storyline of Brian and Jennifer's, they are headed for a collision course if something does not change rather quickly in their priorities. Take a minute to sort through the following questions as they relate to this story. As you do, be open to something that might stand out that could relate to your story.

1. What initial step of action could Jennifer take to help get Brian on the same page with her regarding home life?

2. What advice would you give this couple to help them avoid a possible storm that could easily leave them both very wounded?

3. Do you see your own life/marriage/family in Brian and Jennifer's story? If yes, in what ways? What actions/steps are you taking to help your family avoid a similar pitfall?

I am a firm believer that prioritizing your marriage and family is a decision you will never regret. Not only will it allow you to experience great peace and fulfillment within your home, but it is also necessary, allowing you to experience the next step in this journey—"The Power of Connection."

> Once you identify everyone's capacities, you can make much better decisions that benefit everyone in your household.

Making it Personal

- On a scale of 1 to 10, with 1 being your lowest priority, how would you honestly score your marriage relationship? What would your spouse score your marriage?

- For many couples, the tendency is to place the kids as a higher priority than the marriage. Have you found this to be true in your own home? In what ways?

- Take a few moments to write down what your home would look like ideally if your marriage and family were operating on the same page, with the marriage taking first priority.

Chapter 3

The Power of Connection

Chapter 3: The Power of Connection

"So now I am giving you a new commandment: Love each other. Just as I have loved you, you should love each other" (John 13:34).

I believe the most painful of all human emotions is the feeling of being disconnected from the people with whom we share life. It is a fact of life that it is possible to be around people daily and never really know them. This happens in marriages, with our kids, at the workplace, at church, on sports teams, and in clubs and organizations.

As simple as this may seem, part of why we experience disconnection is because we have lost the value of having face-to-face conversations with people. We have given up the value of time spent having heart-to-heart talks in favor of getting more done, sending a text message, or promising each other we will get together soon, while knowing it will likely never happen. In short, we have come to value activity over relationships, and the results are tragic.

> A fact of life is that it is possible to be around people daily and never really know them.

The Front Porch

You do not have to look very far for evidence that supports that we live disconnected lives. For instance, just a few decades ago one would not have dreamed of building a home that did not have a front porch upon which to sit and share conversations. The porch was an indication that you had the intention of spending time on it as a primary place of meaningful communication with family, neighbors, and friends.

The porch (or even a shady spot in the front yard) was where the social media conversations of the day took place. It was where you learned about the rise in gas prices, or the sudden shift of position in a politician's point of view. It was where the funny stories of times past were told and retold that helped you recall your family's heritage. It did not matter if all the stories were true. What mattered was that you were there together with those you loved…unhurried. It was where memories were made and life connections took root.

Some of the fondest memories from my childhood are when my family would visit my grandparents. Their house was on a dirt road in the country. They had a full-length front porch and a few shade trees in the yard that cooled the air just enough even in the dead heat of summer that we could enjoy a glass of tea as we engaged in conversation.

Today, a front porch is, at best, a place for ferns and the deacon's bench that was purchased at a yard sale. In our day-to-day life of going to work, picking up the kids, and getting the science project finished on time, we have just enough time to walk across the porch; that's about it.

Obviously, it is far more than just a structure on a house, or whether there are shade trees in the front yard, that we are concerned with. The goal is to find ways to connect with those closest to us. I want to offer several suggested starting places for reconnecting with the people you love and care about the most.

Reconnecting with Your Spouse

To make strides in reconnecting with your spouse, I recommend using the Twenty Second Rule. That is, make it a point each day to give each other a meaningful, non-sexual hug or embrace for at least twenty seconds. While this may seem elementary, research shows that significant bonding takes place between two people when giving each other something as simple as a twenty-second hug.

According to an article found in USA Today, "Loving contact before a tough day at work 'could carry over and protect you throughout the day,' says psychologist Karen Grewen with the School of Medicine at the University of North Carolina-Chapel Hill." The article goes on to state, according to Tiffany Field of the Touch Research Institute at the University of Miami Medical School, "Touch lowers output of cortisol, a stress hormone. When cortisol dips, there's a surge of two 'feel good' brain chemicals, serotonin and dopamine." You may have a full calendar, but a daily hug should be a bare minimum for strengthening your most important human relationship! So go ahead—put the book down and give it a try!

● Second, it is important to include all of your senses when engaging in conversation. This may seem impossible, but forming the habit of focusing completely on one another, even if it is only for a short time each day, pays great dividends. You may have to turn off the TV, go into a room separate from the kids, turn off your electronic devices, or shut out other possible distractions to let your companion have your undivided attention. Look them in the eyes, listen with your ears and heart, and be close enough to hold their hand. Over time, these small steps of action will help you develop a soulful connection that most couples used to enjoy but have taken for granted as the years have passed them by.

> You may have to turn off the TV, go into a room separate from the kids, turn off your electronic devices, or shut out other possible distractions to let your companion have your undivided attention.

This simple daily routine has become a type of necessary glue for my wife and me. While it may sound old-fashioned—like something you would have seen in a family-oriented sitcom at the end of each day, this is how we try to decompress and reconnect our hearts after life has tried its best to wear us out.

Third, prioritize your calendar in a way that best supports your family instead of allowing the school, business, church, or peers to always decide your family's whereabouts. This is made possible by implementing a few basic calendar rules of thumb:

- **Limit the number of activities your children are involved in.** For example, our kids are each allowed to be involved in one extracurricular activity at a time each semester. One of the greatest decisions you can make as a parent is to stop trying to make your child the world's greatest athlete at age six at the expense of your marriage and family's well-being—not to mention your wallet.

There is plenty of time to expose your children to different learning opportunities without becoming your child's valet service every day to two or three different venues. The truth is that most parents who are overly passionate about their kids being involved in everything simply do not want their kids to miss out on anything, and they want to look like good parents. It is all well-meaning, but the marriage ends up at risk at the hands of the kid's calendar. And the kids do not always get the experience the parents wanted them to have.

- **Set a bedtime for the kids and stick to it.** Nothing will drain your energy more than always feeling like your kids are in your face demanding something. Put them to bed as early as needed so that you can regroup before the start of another day. We try our best to keep a consistent bedtime of 9 p.m. during weekdays and between 10 and 11 p.m. on weekends, depending on what we have going on. A well-rested family is far more capable of handling the ongoing stresses of life than a family that is strewn from one place to the next and surviving on minimal sleep.

- **Schedule times to be together as a couple.** Believe it or not, even a short run to the grocery store together without the kids can do amazing things for you as a couple. Go catch a movie, eat a favorite dessert, take a walk, plan a trip to the place you both have always wanted to go. Find a sitter for the kids somewhere away from home, order dinner on delivery, and extend your bedroom to your living room. Close the shades, put on a movie, and rekindle your romance. The goal is to find ways of making time for each other so that you are not always operating in crisis mode.

Ironically, the couples with the second highest divorce rate in the US are couples who have been married for twenty years or longer. The reason, while complex, is quite simple to explain. Couples spend the first eighteen years raising children. In the process, they unintentionally fail to continuously nurture the friendship within the marriage, and before they know it the kids have taken center stage in the home. One day out of the blue, once the kids are grown and out of the house, one spouse takes a look at the other and says, "Who are you?" The rest of the story is found in the record books at your local courthouse.

> The goal is to find ways of making time for each other so that you are not always operating in crisis mode.

- **Slow down. I mean, really slow down!** Be determined to live with less, if it allows you to enjoy life and not just survive it. The problem with affluence in our culture is that we live as fast and as busy as our money will allow. We often go and do because we can, not because we should.

  Instead, take time to notice sunsets. Embrace the miracle of having kids running around. Let yourself laugh more. Try something new. Invite those friends over whom you have been putting off for so long because you have "been busy." Slow down.

Reconnecting with Your Kids

Recognizing that the word *kids* can refer to an infant or grown adult depending on one's point of view, I want to focus primarily on connecting with your kids who are school age or younger and still in the home.

- **Make it your daily aim to place high priority on physical touch.** Hug your kids regularly, even if they are the quarterback of the senior high football team. Hold your smaller kids in your lap. Get on the floor and wrestle with them or play dollhouse. They yearn for your affection in this way, and you will set them up to experience healthy social interaction down the road when you get on their level through appropriate physical touch. This also builds your kids' sense of trust and safety.

- **Discipline yourself daily to disconnect completely from your world in order to enter your children's lives individually.** This is a tough one, but your friend's text or the latest social media post is not nearly as important as your child's need to know they are noticed, that they are the apple of your eye, and that they have your undivided attention. Most kids with siblings already feel like they have to compete for mom's or dad's attention. Setting a goal of giving five minutes a day of focused time to each child when possible is a great starting point for handling this demand.

> A time is soon coming when you will give anything to enter your child's world, but they will have moved into another phase of life.

During younger stages of life leading up to adolescence, your kids will constantly invite you into their orbit to play, to watch them dance, or to hear them sing. Do everything in your power to oblige them. If you are truly in the middle of something and cannot give them the immediate attention they desire, give them a time frame within reason when you will be available—and stick to it!

Also, be willing to do what they want to do, not just the activities that you enjoy. Some of the most self-centered people on the planet are parents who will not prioritize their kid's dreams and desires ahead of their own. This happens especially when the child's dreams and desires fail to line up with what the parent wants to spend their time doing. A time is soon coming when you will give anything to enter your child's world, but they will have moved into another phase of life. Now is the time we have to act.

- **Schedule fun times for your family.** While some families can afford a week or two away each year for vacation, you will be surprised what a minimally planned half-day trip to the local swimming hole will do for your household. My family often enjoys a thirty-minute drive to a no-cost, clean recreational area where we can unplug from the world and just be together for a relaxing and enjoyable time. You cannot consistently operate out of demand and responsibility. Building fun times into your routine can help alleviate stress and help you stay connected as a family unit like nothing else can.

- **Take time to listen to what your kids are telling you.** Most of the problems they will want to talk about will not have clear solutions; let them talk anyway. They just need to know you care as you listen with your eyes as well as your ears.

- **We need to be willing to admit when we make mistakes and seek immediate forgiveness when we have wronged our children.** The best way to teach our children how to right their wrongs with others is to right our wrongs with them when we blow it. As parents, there is always a tendency to minimize the hurts our kids may be experiencing at any given time. From a harsh word spoken to them at school to the disappointing loss of a favorite pet, our kids experience a lot of pain growing up. Regrettably, some of the pain will come from us. Rather than treating our children's wounds as if they do not exist or as if they really are not that big of a deal, we need to stop and listen to their story. We need to try our best to see the pain or problem from their perspective, through their eyes. We can then model empathy, compassion, and understanding, which are the tools they will need for all of their future relationships. We can also help by making things right if we have been the ones in the wrong.

This takes courage and emotional strength as parents; but if we will choose to humble ourselves and model this correctly, we can set them up to enter adulthood with minimal negative baggage left over from their home of origin and give them the ability to succeed in their life's most important relationships one day with a family of their own. Refuse to do this and you will set them up to always find someone else to blame for their mistakes, and you as their parents will most likely be the names at the top of their list.

I must admit that one of the hardest things to do at times as a parent is to have to admit to my kids when I have made a mistake. Of the many, many times I have had to go and make things right with one of my kids for something I have said or done that hurt them, I can recall one situation in particular when I used an angry tone to correct my son in public. Is there anything worse than looking back at how you screwed up as a parent—in front of other people you know? Well, thankfully, on this occasion I practiced what I am trying to convey. I went to my son privately, not long after the incident occurred, and tried my best to make things right. I didn't go to him and say, "Son, if I have done anything to hurt you, I am sorry." Rather, I held him close to me and specifically acknowledged my fault of using an angry tone and embarrassing my son in the presence of other people. Then I shared with him how I should have handled the situation and asked for his forgiveness. As parents, the goal should always be doing whatever it takes to keep the air clear and our hearts connected with our kids, even when it means admitting our mistakes.

> As parents, the goal should always be doing whatever it takes to keep the air clear and our hearts connected with our kids, even when it means admitting to our mistakes.

- **We must do everything in our power to avoid the costly mistake of giving our kids everything they want at the expense of not giving them the gift of ourselves.** Toys, cars, and gadgets will never suffice in place of your undivided love and attention, your daily affection, and the assurance of knowing you are there for your children. It does not mean we have to attend every single thing they do. It means that we are there regularly cheering them on, supporting them, and being there when they need us.

As simple as it seems, we cannot allow ourselves to remain on the stage as a bunch of dancing chickens, going everywhere and doing everything everyone thinks we should, if we are serious about being there for our spouse and kids. So far, we have recognized that our fast-paced culture has led many of us to live disconnected lives from those we love the most. We have also discovered practical ways to reconnect daily with our spouse and children. Take a minute to consider the following questions, and then we will get our grasp on "The Power of a Well-Kept Heart."

Making It Personal

- What are the primary causes of the lack of personal connection you have had recently with your spouse and children?

- What do you anticipate will be the hardest of the four action steps to put into practice with your spouse? Why?

- What do your children need the most from you right now?

Chapter 4

The Power of a Well-Kept Heart

Chapter 4: The Power of a Well-Kept Heart

"Guard your heart above all else, for it determines the course of your life" (Proverbs 4:23).

When I hear the word *discipline*, I tend to cringe a bit. I mentally return to my baseball-playing days of spending long hours in the heat, running until I thought my legs would fall off, and doing drills until I could perform them in my sleep. I do not have a desire to relive those days at this point in my life's journey. On the other hand, I do recall the tremendous rewards that came with being in great physical condition, and getting to play on several championship-level teams from Pee Wee at age six to Division 1 college baseball at age twenty.

If our goal is to live closely connected lives with those we love and care about the most and to get off the stage as a dancing chicken, we must recognize the importance of self-discipline, but from a slightly different angle. Allow me to introduce to you the discipline of a well-kept heart. We grow up in a world that is passionate about teaching you how to manage your time, your budget, your tasks, and the people around you. Sadly, most of us are not given a course in how to manage our hearts, and I am not talking about the muscle in the center of your chest cavity. I am referring to the core of who you are as a person—your mind, will, and emotions.

Allow me to explain. A person may receive an A+ for being able to efficiently check things off on their daily planner, but receive an F in the category of heart management that same day by ignoring growing feelings of resentment toward their spouse and choosing not to discuss those feelings. Someone may receive all kinds of recognition from their company for being the person who goes the extra mile in limitless personal sacrifices for the team. But what do they profit in the end if, beneath their endless sacrifices, they have feelings of being taken advantage of by their boss and a deep hatred for their job? The Bible puts it this way in Matthew 16:26: "And what do you benefit if you gain the whole world but lose your own soul? Is anything worth more than your soul?"

With that said, there are two broad categories in which most of us have plenty of room for growth when it comes to having a well-kept heart. They include rediscovering the lost art of contentment and the need for self-care.

The Lost Art of Contentment

When choosing how to spend your time, most of us cannot ignore the reality of having to work and earn an income. It seems that in our culture, we find ourselves in one of three categories regarding careers. Unless you enter a six or seven-digit salaried occupation, you can climb the corporate ladder and settle for only the highest paying opportunities that come your way. You can accept the option of lesser paying opportunities that do not provide the big bonuses, but afford you more time at home. Or you may find yourself maxed out on time and energy in low income jobs with little opportunity for advancement or little resources to better yourself. There does not seem to be a viable blend of options on the menu.

Without trying to dig too deep into the factors shaping your current standard of living, I want to present an option that is available to you that really does not depend on how much you make or what your title is, but can have an enormous effect on your personal well-being. Admittedly it is a much less marketed way to go. It's a road less traveled and will really test the motivation behind why you do what you do. It is called contentment. Contentment is the arch enemy of our modern day approach to making a living. In the eyes of some, contentment settles for average and takes the zeal out of pursuing the American Dream. On the flip side, however, contentment could also be your very best ally for creating a home environment that thrives and flourishes in connectivity, which is the new dream you are embracing anyway. Instead of just striving to make a living, it can set you up to make a life!

> **Contentment is the archenemy of our modern-day approach to making a living.**

Contentment is a broad enough term—one in which all of us can find satisfaction, if we truly want to keep a well-kept heart. Contentment helps you keep life in proper perspective and prioritizes the heart of your family like nothing else. It does not have to necessarily mean accepting less pay as much as it means putting up necessary boundaries so that your closest relationships are not in danger of being sacrificed on the altar of needing to have more stuff. This is hard, especially if you are used to getting what you want when you want it without having to develop a finer filter that separates wants from legitimate needs.

Contentment is also made difficult by the fact that we are more prone to keep in step with every trendy phase our culture promotes than to risk looking like we are behind. This is where we are really tempted to hop back on the stage and perform for the people around us. Men, for example, do not want their spouse to drive a less than perfect-looking vehicle for fear that it would be a reflection on their ability to provide, even if a less-modern vehicle in great running condition for a much cheaper price was available. Parents do not want their kids in hand-me-downs when their friends are wearing the latest fashions, for fear that their kids might feel less than they are. The list could go on.

No More Dancing Chickens

While there is certainly nothing wrong with owning newer and nicer things, and while you always need to be sensitive to the needs and desires of your family, the majority of your financial decisions can easily come from a faulty belief system that says the more you have and the nicer it is, the more important of a person you are. I say, "Enough already!" It is time to make changes, and finding contentment is a stepping stone in the right direction of staying off the stage as a dancing chicken for good. It is a decision that probably will not get you invited to as many Christmas parties, but it will set your family up for experiencing the gift of closeness like you have never known before—when your priority becomes one another instead of things.

Learning the art of contentment can begin with something as simple as being thankful for the little things in life that are afforded to you every day. Things like food, clothing, and shelter are not a given for the majority of the world. One major challenge we all face as parents is to instill a grateful attitude and spirit within our children. I know of no better way to instill this indispensable quality than to model gratitude in front of them. My wife and I attempt to do this each day as we are reminded of the many blessings we have been given. We often fail, but we keep this in front of us as our goal. It is also such a rewarding experience as a parent to hear your children following suit and expressing gratitude for the little things in life that are so easily taken for granted. This requires intentionality of heart and remaining focused on the right things.

Another way to recover the art of contentment in your home is to become aware of the needs around you and model for your children what it means to lend a helping hand to the less fortunate. My wife and I are constantly challenged by our kids wanting the latest and greatest gadget that "everyone else" already has. We do our best to combat this by reminding our kids of the many things they already have. We also encourage them to contribute to needs of others as they become aware of them on their own. Now it seems we find ourselves having to give proper parameters to our kids for what they can and cannot give away to others in need. It is a much better problem to have, even though we definitely are not out of the woods in battling a "must have it now" mentality.

> Learning the art of contentment can begin with something as simple as being thankful for the little things in life that are afforded to you every day.

A third way of making contentment your aim is to develop patience in spending. Patience is the biggest enemy to the consumer who cannot function if they are not out buying something. However, patience does give you time to evaluate the purpose of your next purchase. Here are a few basic questions to ask before buying that next "must have" item:

- Is this item a legitimate need or a want?

- Can I buy the item without skipping out on bills that need to be paid?

- Can I buy this item without having to go into debt?

- Am I attempting to fill some sort of personal void in my life by purchasing this item?

- If I buy this item, what will it say to my children about my value system?

The need to recover an attitude and mindset of gratitude cannot be overstated. For every item we think we need, there is an item we already have that we just need to be thankful for. It may be helpful before moving on to just sit down and make a list of the many ways your life has already been blessed. Then share some things on your list with your family. Before you know it, that must-have item may not seem to be such an urgent need after all.

The Need for Self-Care

Another vital part of having a well-kept heart and staying off the performance stage involves self-care. I have heard self-care described by different people as listening to what your life is telling you. Most people manage their life the same way they manage their vehicles: they go full speed every day and do not service them unless something breaks, comes loose, or quits. They go and go and go until they have an anxiety attack or have to be put on medicine to help them cope with the pace of life they have chosen to live.

> Most people manage their lives the same way they manage their vehicles: they go full speed every day and do not service them unless something breaks, comes loose, or quits.

People from all walks of life also tend to lean toward two extremes—living self-centered, self-absorbed lives with little concern for anyone else or burying themselves in doing for others at the neglect of their own hearts. The first group misses out on the joy of serving others. The latter group ends up bitter when "others" they are serving are not seemingly willing to go to the same extreme to serve them in return. Neither side lends itself to your goal of building lasting connections with those closest to you.

A couple of years ago, I was one who was very guilty of burying myself in doing things for others at the neglect of my own heart. What started off as a genuine, healthy desire to serve my local church became an all-consuming passion that, having gone unchecked for a period of time, eventually led me down a road of heartache. Over time, it became clear that I was in way over my head in service to others at the neglect of my heart; instead of serving from a heart of gratitude, I eventually served from a heart of resentment and fatigue. This had lasting effects on me and my family and it took a while to recognize what it was doing to us. Sometimes you just cannot clearly see what is happening to you while you are in certain situations. I am now back serving regularly in a local church, but this time it is with the right perspective and in a much healthier balance for me and for my family.

The best-selling book of all time, the Bible, even makes reference to caring for ourselves in what is referred to as the second greatest of all the commandments. It says in Matthew 22:39, "Love your neighbor as yourself." People in the faith community tend to hold high the banner of loving your neighbor and often have a complete misunderstanding of the rest of the phrase, "as yourself."

The "love your neighbor" part makes us feel good on the inside when we think we can make a difference in someone else's life. However, all too often the "as yourself" part gets buried beneath a false sense of guilt, believing that anything you do for yourself must be wrong and self-centered. Yet this was never the intention of this teaching. At the end of the day, you cannot love your neighbor adequately if you do not have a healthy love and care for your own personal well-being.

> You need a plan for ongoing personal renewal so that your service to others is fueled by love instead of guilt.

You need a plan for ongoing personal renewal so that your service to others is fueled by love instead of guilt. What I am describing is self-care. Here are a few basic starting points for consideration.

Steps to Self-Care

First, begin by identifying what replenishes your tank—your mental, physical, emotional, and spiritual well-being—and put it into action today. You may enjoy reading, taking a leisure walk, praying or meditating, taking a short nap, or having coffee with a close friend as a way to regain your sense of vitality. Start with committing small increments of time each day to what fills you up, and realize that the more demanding your schedule is, the more time you will eventually need to invest filling up your tank to avoid running on empty.

I typically fill my tank on a daily basis by sitting on the front porch in my rocking chair in the early mornings or late evenings reading a good book and watching the squirrels jump from tree to tree in the yard. I also love to work in the yard raking leaves or attempting to do some landscaping. My absolute favorite tank-filler of all is going camping on the Buffalo River and having meaningless conversations with a few buddies around the campfire. What fills your tank? Make it a priority, and take the time to do it.

Second, get more rest. Every seven days, take a complete day off from work mentally, emotionally, and physically. No matter your occupation, if you cannot take a twenty-four hour period away from it on a weekly basis, you need to consider searching for a different job. It doesn't have to be from seven in the morning to seven the next morning. It may be from five in the evening to five in the evening the next day. While there are a select few careers that may have occasional prolonged periods without rest, the majority of employers honor a twenty-four hour day off within a seven-day time period. Your health requires it, and if you do not take time off now, chances are your body will require you to take time off later in a hospital bed. It will probably come at the most inconvenient time of your life and will be far less economical.

Just because you end up with thirty minutes of extra time in the afternoon does not mean you need to spend it on an activity. Instead of running from free time, begin to embrace it as your friend and let yourself feel good about doing nothing. This can be a real challenge, especially if you grew up in a home that honored activity and frowned on the idea of rest. Learning how to refill your tank through proper rest can become a true game changer if you will stick to it and make it a part of your routine.

> To offer the best you to those you love and care about the most, begin today taking steps toward the changes needed for a more successful you.

Third, pay attention to your food choices. I recognize I am hitting this broadly, but if you constantly find yourself complaining of feeling exhausted, chances are you are dropping the ball in the food and beverage department. As simple examples, consider drinking more water and fewer sodas or energy drinks; eat less junk food and more fruits and veggies. You have heard this all of your life! But as you grow older, these little things really begin to matter. Changing poor eating habits not only helps reduce weight gain but will also replenish your energy levels to what you require in order to match the demands of each day. Healthier foods will do this in a much healthier and more lasting way than a caffeine rush or a candy bar.

Fourth, incorporate a natural regimen of exercise to your day. I know. I used the "E" word. Just remember: Exercise equals more available energy. A consistent form of exercise that keeps the heart rate up for at least thirty minutes three times a week can greatly reduce the risk of heart disease and provide your body with the fuel you need to make it through your day, without having to poison it with products that are wrapped in a cool label. For me personally, I have started running again. I used to do this for athletics. Now I do this out of necessity so that my body does not absorb all of the stress of my daily life.

Most importantly, understand that your closest relationships are being affected by how well you take care of yourself in each of the areas mentioned. To offer the best you to those you love and care about the most, begin today taking steps toward the changes needed for a more successful you.

You will begin to notice a significant difference in your ability to live free from the unhealthy expectations of others when you adopt the discipline of a well-kept heart into your daily routines. Find contentment in what you can afford, and listen to what your life is telling you without feeling guilty about it. There is another key ingredient left that, when acted upon, has the ability to get you over the top and well on your way to connected living. It is "The Power of Believing."

Making It Personal

- Is a lack of contentment something that needs to be addressed in your personal life and in your home? Why or why not?

- What is a realistic starting point for recovering the lost art of contentment for your family?

- Is self-care an issue for you? Would others who are close to you agree or disagree with your response? What act of self-care do you need to begin today?

Chapter 5

The Power of Believing

Chapter 5: The Power of Believing

"Don't be faithless any longer. Believe!" (John 20:27b)

We have discussed specific pressures from our culture as well as people we know that can have a major impact on your ability to connect (and remain connected) to those you love and care about the most. We have also looked at helpful strategies on how to overcome those pressures and no longer have to live as dancing chickens on the stage of life. For our sake, you could easily call those pressures "enemies from outside the camp." There is another enemy that is perhaps the most dangerous of all that, unless recognized, can continue doing lasting damage to your closest relationships. The enemy is not outside of the camp, but inside. In fact, this enemy lies within each of us.

We are our worst enemy. This is because we are selfish people. None of us are immune to being selfish. At its core, living like a dancing chicken is really nothing more than a life of self-preservation. It may be that you are consumed with living to please people who are controlling you from the outside. But the root of having to please everybody is a self-protecting nature that is very, very self-centered.

> We need a cure for the disease of having to have life our way.

Furthermore, nothing breaks the bond of connection with others like selfishness. We are plagued with this deadly cancer, and because of it we find ourselves extremely limited in our ability to build the

71

kind of lasting connections with our family that our heart is so hungry for. We need a cure for the disease of having to have life our way and living it in the fear of letting everyone down. The grip of self-preservation is so powerful that the cure must come from a source outside of us.

A few years ago, our region was devastated by an ice storm. For several days, our home was without power, and transportation was extremely limited. Our city looked like a ghost town, especially at night. You could drive the main roads from one end of town to the other and not even realize you were driving past large buildings and homes due to the power outage.

Fortunately for us, we had some friends who graciously invited us to stay in their home. What was the difference between their home and ours? Simple. They had a generator, and they were able to produce electricity when other homes remained dark and cold. They had a source outside of their normal connections that provided warmth, shelter, and a weekend of fun memories for all of us who stayed there.

In your personal day-to-day living, you need a source outside of yourself that can give you strength when you are weak, serve as an immovable anchor that you can hang on to through life's storms, and provide the power needed to help you change from the inside out.

It is at this point that I again want to draw from ancient wisdom found in the Bible, which has helped more people than any other book written. We will do well to draw insights from it that can help us face this deadly enemy within us head-on. Why should this matter to us? Because of what we have already established: Life as a dancing chicken is all about living for the expectations of other people, who are as deeply flawed as you are and are not worthy of taking ownership over your heart and life. There is, however, One who is worthy.

Connecting to Our Most Powerful Source

The Bible says there is a person who is not only worthy of your heart and life, He is also the whole reason and purpose for which you were made. His expectations are worthy of your utmost attention, though it is not primarily your performance that He desires most—it is your heart. A relationship with God, unlike a religion or a certain set of rules to follow, is described as the greatest, closest relationship a person can have. As a result of having this relationship, you can become your very best for those you love the most, and there will be no reason for living life as a dancing chicken. Your life's audience becomes an audience of One when God enters the picture. Not only does He become the one person you seek to please for the rest of your life, but through your relationship with Him you can conquer your dark side of self-protection and self-preservation.

> I would not be here today had it not been for his selfless act to come to where I was and take me to where I needed to be—out of harm's way.

God wants you to know Him personally, in a very real way. He, in His infinite wisdom, knew there was nothing we could do to bridge the gap between us and Him to make this relationship possible. He knew we could never do enough good to somehow earn His approval when He looked at our imperfections compared to His sinless perfection. So He took the initiative to be able to relate to us in the most personal way. He sent His Son, Jesus, to live a fully human life on earth as a servant of all men. Not only was He was fully human and came to serve, not to be served, He was also fully God—God in the flesh, in living color.

Jesus came to earth to relate to us personally with His life and to fulfill an even greater mission with His death. Because God could not look favorably upon the sinful wrongdoings of humankind that came from our dark side, it was necessary for Jesus to pay the ultimate penalty of death on a Roman cross in our place. Hebrews 9:22 puts it this way: "In fact, according to the law of Moses, nearly everything was purified with blood. For without the shedding of blood, there is no forgiveness." This death penalty that Jesus fulfilled should have been ours to pay because of our marked tendency to live life our way, apart from our Creator.

This selfless act by Jesus is described this way in 1 Peter 3:18: "Christ suffered for our sins once for all time. He never sinned, but he died for sinners to bring you safely home to God." Did you catch that last phrase? The whole reason Jesus came to earth and took upon Himself the punishment for our selfish acts was so that we could be connected to the God of the universe in a lifelong, life-changing relationship.

This relationship with God can be yours when you understand the power of believing. We use the word *believe* very loosely in our culture. We say, without thinking, that we believe one brand of vehicles is more dependable than another, or we believe one restaurant is better tasting than another. However, the word *believe* is used in a much more powerful way in the Bible.

Take John 3:16, for example. You have probably seen the guy in the end zone of a football game who has John 3:16 painted on a sheet in big red letters and numbers. That is a verse in the Bible that says, "For God loved the world so much that he gave his one and only Son, so that everyone who believes in him will not perish but have eternal life." We will talk more about this verse in a minute.

When I was nine years old, my family went to Galveston, Texas for vacation. While we spent time on the beach, we also enjoyed time at the hotel swimming pool. One scorching hot afternoon I decided to take a swim in the pool, except for me it was more like a wade, because I did not know how to swim.

While my mom was reading a book just a few feet away from where I was playing in the shallow end of the pool, I noticed my inflatable ring drifting toward the deep end. It was almost within arm's reach, so I did what most nine year olds would have done—I lunged for it with all my might. There was only one problem. I missed. For the next few seconds that felt like an eternity, I sank to the bottom of the pool and pushed myself up for air trying to survive.

About that time, I could hear my mom saying, "Son, just come up for air," not realizing the kind of immediate trouble I was in. Thankfully, in a split second, a man sitting near my mom noticed what was happening, threw his newspaper to the side, jumped into the pool, and saved my life. I remember it like it happened this morning. I am not sure exactly how he got me up out of the water so quickly, but I am sure of this: I probably would not be here today had it not been for his selfless act to come to where I was and take me to where I needed to be—out of harm's way.

When the Bible says in John 3:16 that believing in Jesus is the ticket to having eternal life, it is much weightier than just believing He exists or that He was a good teacher. Instead, it is the picture of a spiritually drowning person going down for the third time, when a rescue swimmer reaches into the water and pulls you from certain death. Your response is one of faith—you hold on to them like your very life depended on it. This is what it means to believe in Jesus. It means to take hold of Jesus as your only hope of ever being rescued from serving your lifelong sentence of selfishness, and from the ultimate sentence of death—being separated from a loving God for eternity.

The Bible even goes on to describe how you can begin this relationship with God. It says in Romans 10:10, "For it is by believing in your heart that you are made right with God, and it is by confessing with your mouth that you are saved." The word *saved* is another word for being rescued. Without watering down the meaning of this verse, what God is communicating is that He wants you to have a conversation with Him as a starting point to your relationship with Him.

The idea of having a conversation with a God whom you cannot see may seem tough to even know where to begin. The Bible gives us even more insight into this. In Jeremiah 29:11-14 it says, "'For I know the plans I have for you,' says the LORD. 'They are plans for good and not for disaster, to give you a future and a hope. In those days when you pray, I will listen. If you look for me wholeheartedly, you will find me. I will be found by you," says the LORD.'" The key to beginning a relationship with Creator God is to go after Him with all your heart. If you use this verse as your guide, you can tell God, using everyday language, what you want Him to do for you. It may go something like this:

> "God, I agree that up to this point I have done my best to run my own life apart from You, and it is obvious that I need to resign. I believe in what Your Son Jesus did for me on the cross that no one else was willing or able to do. By accepting His payment for my wrongdoings, I am choosing today to begin my relationship with You. I ask You to help me conquer my dark side of selfishness that plagues my closest relationships, and I ask You to help me connect with the people closest to me like never before. Amen."

If you have just had that conversation with God or one like it, I want to congratulate you on beginning life's most important relationship—the one with God. Just like any other relationship, your relationship with God will need to be nourished and strengthened in order to maintain the kind of close connection you desire to have with Him. I would like to encourage you to consider becoming a part of a Bible-believing local fellowship with people who can come alongside you and help you continue to make strides in your faith adventure. There are even Bible-believing faith groups online which would love to assist you in your newfound faith.

Having a relationship with God is so much more than just having someone to turn to during difficult times or having someone you can treat like a giant Santa Claus in the sky, waiting at your beck and call. Rather, He desires to walk alongside you through your everyday life, giving you wisdom, counsel, and strength for the journey ahead. It is in your relationship with God that you will find "The Power of a Promise Kept."

Making It Personal

- Can you think of different ways that your "enemy within" has hurt your relationships with those closest to you in times past?

76

- Does the idea of having a relationship with God strike you as appealing or as something that, up until now, has seemed completely impossible?

- Does the idea of having a relationship with God versus having a religion about Him make a difference in how you view God?

Chapter 6

The Power of A
Promise Kept

Chapter 6: The Power of a Promise Kept

> "Then Christ will make his home in your hearts as you trust in him. Your roots will grow down into God's love and keep you strong" (Ephesians 3:17).

It may not seem like much at first, but beginning a relationship with Creator God is the most important decision you could ever make. Whether you just expressed your heart to God in a prayer for the first time at the close of the previous chapter or you have been walking in a relationship with God for many years, there are great benefits to being in His company. You need to understand what you get when God enters your life. Among all of the attributes that God will bring to your life in days and years to come, these four attributes are anchors that you will not need to ever turn loose: He gives you a promise, a person, a purpose, and a process. We will take time to look at each one of these individually to get a better grip on how they impact your life.

You need to understand what you get when God enters your life.

A Promise

Having been brought into a relationship with God through faith, you have been granted a very important promise from God. The Bible says in Hebrews 13:5 that God promises, "I will never fail you. I will never abandon you." In another passage of Scripture found in Matthew 28:20, the same promise is guaranteed by Jesus Christ when he says, "And be sure of this: I am with you always, even to the end of the age," and "No, I will not abandon you as orphans—I will come to you" (John 14:18). How could Creator God promise to always be with you and promise to never forsake you? He makes it possible by giving you Himself in the Person of the Holy Spirit.

A Person

When you turn to God in total trust for Him to rescue you spiritually, He not only forgives the wrongdoings from your dark side—past, present, and future—but He also sends His Holy Spirit to live inside you. This is how He keeps His promise to always be with you no matter what. The Holy Spirit is not a force or influence. He is not a denomination, a set of religious beliefs, or an annual tradition to be celebrated. He is a Person, and He has a vital role to play in your life as one who is striving to no longer live life as a dancing chicken.

In John 14:16-17, Jesus says, "I will ask the Father, and he will give you another Advocate, who will never leave you. He is the Holy Spirit, who leads into all truth. The world cannot receive him, because it isn't looking for him and doesn't recognize him. But you know him, because he lives with you now and later will be in you." This teaching of the Holy Spirit living inside of you as a believer is supported in other key passages in the Bible, including 1 Corinthians 3:16, "Don't you realize that all of you together are the temple of God and that the Spirit of God lives in you?" and continued in 2 Corinthians 6:16, "For we are the temple of the living God." Again, in Ephesians 1:13, we read, "And now you Gentiles have also heard the truth, the Good News that God saves you. And when you believed in Christ, he identified you as his own by giving you the Holy Spirit, whom he promised long ago."

A glorious mystery, the teaching of the indwelling Holy Spirit is one that cannot be ignored or set aside if you are serious about having a relationship with God and learning to follow His plan for your life.

As the Holy Spirit lives inside you as your most trusted Counselor, He gently nudges you in the right direction to please God and to love those closest to you. The longer you live in this faith, the more clearly His voice and leadership will be understood deep in your heart as you carry on in your everyday life.

In John 16:13, we read, "When the Spirit of truth comes, he will guide you into all truth." The truth referred to in this verse is the truth found in the Bible. From now until you pass from this earth, God's desire is to align your life with the truth of His word so that you can learn to please God in every way. God does this by shaping your character into His. God is in the process of changing you from the inside out—from a selfish, self-protective person to a person with a heart to serve others out of pure motives. When your relationship with God becomes the center point and focus of your life, things begin to change! It is His work in you that sets your heart free from self and empowers you to love others better and more strongly than ever.

It is not just God doing the work in you to bring about needed change. It is also you learning to cooperate with God as He works in your life through His Holy Spirit. What are some of the changes that God desires to accomplish in your life as a result of you having begun a relationship with Him? Furthermore, how can your relationship with God affect your relationships with those closest to you?

A Purpose

A few weeks ago, my son was motivated by a creative spark to build something in his bedroom using PVC pipe about ten feet in length. Only heaven knows what his final project was to look like or become, but he was adamant that the pipe would have to be cut in half before it could do him any good. So he did what many a good twelve-year old boys would do in his situation where tools were scarce and time was short— he tried using a file as a hand saw for cutting the pipe. If this story sounds unusual or alarms you in any way, your concerns would soon be put to rest if you knew how safe and low-key this project attempt was compared to some of the other daring ideas my son has come up with in recent years.

He began sawing away at the pipe using the file, which was actually intended for removing sharp edges from metal objects. Suffice it to say, after a long and arduous effort to cut the pipe in half, my son eventually reached his goal. About that time, my wife discovered him in his room. He was worn out from his hard labor. She asked him what he was trying to do with the file, and then gently broke the news to him that cutting PVC pipe was not the intended purpose for the file. He will hopefully remember that lesson the next time his creativity requires an actual saw.

Unfortunately, we are guilty of approaching our lives the same way as my son approached his desire to cut the pipe. Without having God at the center of your life, you will go about your day-to-day business with the faulty understanding that the purpose of your life is to please you—your desires, your happiness, and your agendas—as well as the people watching you dance like a chicken. The results are disastrous. You will end up making a mess of your life, spending a lot of effort creating a life for yourself that you think will bring you lasting happiness. Instead, you will end up feeling less fulfilled than before and move further away from the people you were put on earth to love unconditionally and selflessly. To draw from the illustration in the previous chapter of a drowning person needing a lifeguard, without Christ you will go through life doing everything you possibly can to keep your head above water, even if it means pulling others down in the process so you can stay alive. It is not unusual for someone who is drowning to put up a fight and even take people under with them, thereby hurting the one who is trying to save them from certain death.

We are focused on watching out for number one, and we will go to the mat with just about anyone who tries to tell us to do otherwise. Are you beginning to see how badly we need a Savior, a rescuer, and how badly we must understand the new purpose God has for us in this life that is much bigger than just living for ourselves?

As a person following after God and His will for your life, you now have a new purpose. No longer is your purpose to satisfy yourself at every turn. Rather, it is to please God and honor Him in how you live. You exist to serve and to please God. The good news is that He provides a clear plan in His written Word for how to go about living this kind of life.

God will use the rest of your earthly life to reach His ultimate goal, which is to shape your will and your character in such a way that you will reflect the life of His Son, Jesus, as much as possible during your time on the earth. His Son, Jesus, lived to please the Father in every way by constantly conforming His will to the Father's plans. It is through this process of becoming more like Jesus that you will learn how to truly love your family with a God-sized kind of love that does not come from you only, but from God through you to the world around you.

> How long will it take God to transform your life in such a way that you desire to please Him and live for Him as your One and only audience? The answer is—the rest of your life.

A Process

Few great things are created on a whim. History tells us that it took Michelangelo just over four years to paint the Sistine Chapel. All sections of the Great Wall of China, including some barely visible ruins of the first wall and remains of walls built by successive dynasties, were built over a period of more than 2,000 years between the eighth century BC and the seventeenth century. It took 100,000 oppressed slaves twenty years to build the Great Pyramid of Giza (around 2560 BC). How long will it take God to transform your life in such a way that you desire to please Him and live for Him as your One and only audience? The answer is—the rest of your life.

Here is a simple illustration describing how God does things—He is very committed to setting up a construction site inside your heart when you invite Him to dwell there. As a result, you are a work in progress. It would not be far from accurate for us to wear a shirt that says, in effect, "Please be patient. I will be under construction for the next fifty years." While this may seem more than a little uncomfortable to think of God choosing to shape the character of our lives from the inside out, the truth of the matter is that He does it out of His love for us. He is the greatest foreman of all time, knowing His blueprint for us by heart and exactly what it will take to mold us into the people He created us to be. Our job is to cooperate with Him in the process. The Bible describes this process as that of a potter shaping clay. The prophet Jeremiah wrote this first-person account of his conversation with God:

> So I did as he told me and found the potter working at his wheel. But the jar he was making did not turn out as he had hoped, so he crushed it into a lump of clay again and started over. Then the Lord gave me this message: "O Israel, can I not do to you as this potter has done to his clay? As the clay is in the potter's hand, so are you in my hand" (Jeremiah 18:3-6).

He is calling you to be available to Him for a no-matter-what kind of commitment to follow Him.

Our job is to learn to cooperate with God as He leads us through life, shaping our character and transforming us into a person He can use for His purposes. What I am describing is nothing less than a surrendered life. I will never forget sitting in a worship service at a local church as a young college student when I sensed God speak to me in a very clear way. He said, "All I want is someone who is willing." It was spoken to the deepest parts of my heart. It was personal. It was intentional. It was life-changing. God was calling me to be a willing vessel—a willing, yielded clay pot who would say *yes* to whatever God wanted to do in and through my life. His call and desire for you is no different. Yes, God will likely lead us down different paths, but His overall plan is the same.

He is calling you to be available to Him for a no-matter-what kind of commitment to follow Him. What will your answer be?

A New Heart

As mentioned, God is in the construction business, and His first plan of action is to give you a new heart. This is described by God Himself in Ezekiel 36:26-27: "And I will give you a new heart, and I will put a new spirit in you. I will take out your stony, stubborn heart and give you a tender, responsive heart. And I will put my Spirit in you so that you will follow my decrees and be careful to obey my regulations." God accomplishes this new heart transplant the moment you turn your life over to Him in faith and invite Him to take control of the wheel. A new heart is not something you can go out and earn, nor is it something you can manufacture out of human effort by attending church every week or trying your best to avoid the really big sins. It comes with giving God your life in full surrender. Having a new heart is such an important matter to God because the heart is central to everything you do. God is after your heart. He does not simply want to get you to conform outwardly to a set of religious rules or beliefs or simply ask you to work hard to modify some of your behavior.

This heart surgery by God that I am describing is deeply purposed in God's desire to dwell inside of you by His Spirit and to set your life (in the form of your deepest desires) on a totally different path than the one you have previously followed. His new path for you is one that will be pleasing to Him. He wants a new home to live in, and the old heart of stone will not suffice. It is from your new heart that God will launch the biggest construction project ever, so that you can become everything God intended you to become upon His very first thought of bringing you into the world.

The Need for a New Beginning

Along with giving you a new heart, God's plan of action that actually happens simultaneously is this—He gives you a new beginning. What is it like to have a new beginning, with a new God-indwelled heart, as opposed to your old hardened, self-centered heart and a sinful past hanging over you? It is the difference between being grungy on the inside and being *clean*. Remember God's promise in the book of Ezekiel to give you a new heart? In that same passage, the Lord also says, "I will sprinkle clean water on you, and you will be clean. Your filth will be washed away, and you will no longer worship idols" (Ezekiel 36:25). Before God rescues you from a life filled with self-serving and self-pleasing motives, your heart and mine is filled with all kinds of things that pollute us and make us unclean before a holy God.

For some of us, depending on when we were rescued by Jesus, we may have had an encyclopedia full of skeletons from our past and regrets a mile long that we needed Jesus to forgive and clean up. Even those of us who may not consider ourselves to have had a long history of what we would normally categorize as "the really bad stuff" still had ugly sins of selfishness and pride that came with being the rulers of our own domain apart from God. The Bible says it this way: "For everyone has sinned; we all fall short of God's glorious standard" (Romans 3:23). To *fall short* simply means this—it is the picture of someone aiming an arrow at a target in the distance, and no matter how many times they try to hit the target with their best intentions and effort, they continue missing the mark. When we begin to recognize this about ourselves, we begin to realize how our best efforts just do not add up to a life that is pleasing to God. We may begin to experience feelings of guilt and remorse for the things we have said or done that, before now, we may have never really given much thought. Now, however, with God's Spirit living inside of you, you know your former way of living was not pleasing to Him, and you are no longer satisfied living the way you always have.

Watching Out for Pitfalls

A by-product of God restoring a pure heart inside of you is Him also giving you the ability to recognize and avoid pitfalls that can send you down the slippery slope of a self-serving, self-absorbed life like the one you previously lived (at least to some degree) before Jesus entered the picture. While everyone's story is different in how God worked in your heart to draw you into a relationship with Him, one common thread can be found in all of our stories—we still have the capacity to fail even after we give our lives completely to Him.

We have weaknesses. We have pitfalls uniquely fitted to our weaknesses. We do not test out of all of our struggles with sin and temptation the moment we trust Christ to rescue us from an eternity without God. Granted, you now have the Spirit of God living in you and sin is no longer to be your master; but you are just as prone to make choices that dishonor God as you were before you met Him. The difference is that you do not *have* to do the things your flesh wants to do. You now have the *option* to live for God, and you have access to the power you need to do so.

How do I know about potential pitfalls that exist after giving your life over to God? I have experienced firsthand what it is like to lose some critical battles within my heart that have left me feeling very discouraged in my relationship with God.

> You now have the *option* to live for God, and you have access to the power you need to do so.

There have been times I felt like I had to start all over again from square one. It was not the fact that my heart had gone bad or that the work of God in my life was being wasted or failed somehow. It was mostly due to a lack of spiritual maturity on my part. As I look back on some of my worst of times as a Christian, I now realize that the main cause of me stumbling back into some old sins and habits occasionally was the absence of any real spiritual discipline cultivated in my life. This happens so subtly within us.

From repeated and painful failures, God has brought me to a place of learning some of the most important lessons that have anchored me in my walk with Him. It is certainly not that I am now beyond these lessons, but instead that they have become my companions serving to guide me in this walk of faith. I pray these seven biblical truths will be valuable to you as well as you continue to seek the Lord with all of your heart.

First, it is vitally important that you understand that failure is an event, not a person. Proverbs 24:16 says, "The godly may trip seven times, but they will get up again." This has been a lesson my father sought to instill in me from as early as I can remember, but it has never been more important to remember than in my years as an adult.

Second, your failures are never a surprise to God. His mercy is new every morning, and His grace is greater than all of your mistakes combined. Romans 5:20 says, "God's law was given so that all people could see how sinful they were. But as people sinned more and more, God's wonderful grace became more abundant."

Third, while sin brings with it a variety of consequences that God does not always protect us from, God's plan is to continue providing a road of hope and healing for the most damaged of hearts. "He heals the brokenhearted and bandages their wounds" (Psalms 147:3).

> God's plan is to continue providing a road of hope and healing for the most damaged of hearts.

Fourth, it is often more difficult to forgive oneself for failure than to forgive others when they have failed you. However, if God in His perfect character has chosen to forgive you, who are you to not forgive yourself? Are you more righteous than God? Psalms 130:3-4 says, "Lord, if you kept a record of our sins, who, O Lord, could ever survive? But you offer forgiveness, that we might learn to fear you."

Fifth, though God promises to erase from His memory all of our wrongdoings, He never promises to give us the ability to completely erase our wrongdoings from *our* memory. I believe this is so we will remember how miserable life can be when we are tempted to step out of His plan for us again. In essence, our hurtful memories of personal sin can serve as a schoolmaster to help keep us from wandering off again spiritually. There is much to be learned from the past.

In 1 Corinthians 10, the Bible gives several examples of how God's people in times past experienced His discipline due to straying from His commands. Verse 6 picks up from there and says, "These things happened as a warning to us, so that we would not crave evil things as they did." Your sinful past need not keep you from growing in your relationship with God, but it should serve as a warning of what life was like apart from close fellowship with Jesus.

Sixth, there are times when God chooses to bring transformation and healing to people's lives overnight, while at other times, God chooses to transform you incrementally over several years of walking with Him. This has been more my experience than any other. We are reminded in Romans 12:2, "Don't copy the behavior and customs of this world, but let God transform you into a new person by changing the way you think." The word *transform* is from the same word as *morph*. When I think of the word *morph*, I cannot help but to picture in my mind a butterfly and the process it goes through before we see its true beauty. God's desire is that we would continue to morph into His image as we learn to walk with Him day by day.

> Instead of allowing your past to prevent you from reaching your potential, allow God to use it as a launch pad to use you in ways you could have never have imagined!

Seventh, your biggest weaknesses and failures of times past can become your greatest strengths if you will allow God to use them to reshape your character. They can also become an incredible launch pad for spiritual effectiveness and influence if you learn from them. I am reminded of the apostle Paul who received a thorn in his flesh after receiving direct insights from God that no one could fathom. Here is how Paul describes his thorn in 2 Corinthians 12:7. "So to keep me from becoming proud, I was given a thorn in my flesh, a messenger from Satan to torment me and keep me from becoming proud. Three different times I begged the Lord to take it away. Each time he said, 'My grace is all you need. My power works best in weakness.' So now I am glad to boast about my weaknesses, so that the power of Christ can work through me." Even the great man Paul—who was responsible for writing most of the New Testament and was the greatest missionary of all time second only to Jesus—had a thorn in his flesh that God simply would not allow him to be free from. It was through Paul's weakness that God showed His greatness. Instead of allowing your past to keep you from reaching your potential, allow God to use it as a launch pad to use you in ways you could have never have imagined!

Unbroken Fellowship

God's relationship with you is not based on your ability to be perfect. His Son, Jesus, filled that requirement when He willingly died on the cross as a perfect, spotless sacrifice for my and your personal wrongdoings. However, what God does desire is unbroken fellowship with you. Not only does He desire a clean place to move into (your heart), but He also desires His living quarters to remain pure for the long haul. This is because anything impure that enters your heart grieves His and will keep you from having the kind of close relationship with God for which your heart so hungers and thirsts.

> From now on, you need to think of your sinful acts as pollutants to your heart, where God's Spirit dwells.

Many years ago, my in-laws served as volunteers in our church's student ministry. Not unlike most student ministries, ours had its share of people who loved to pull pranks. My in-laws just happened to be on the receiving end of a prank that would not soon be forgotten. Unknown to them, a group of students had come together, purchased some catfish bait for fishing, and secretly placed it inside the air vents in my in-laws car. Needless to say, the odor from the bait filled the car, and it took my in-laws quite some time to figure out where the stench was coming from.

Once they figured it out and determined who had done this to them, they made sure it would never happen again. Sin pollutes your life like the fish bait polluted my in-laws car, and no one, including the Holy Spirit, wants to dwell in a stench-filled environment. From now on, you need to think of your sinful acts as pollutants to your heart where God's Spirit dwells. His ultimate desire is unbroken fellowship with you, which is made possible when you come to see your personal sin stench the way He does and you no longer allow it to linger in your life.

Not only is it vital for you to start seeing your sin as God does, but you will also greatly benefit from knowing that God's love for you never changes, even when you blow it. When I was around thirteen years of age, I decided I would do my dad a favor by washing his new car in the front yard of my grandparents' house, which was about two and a half hours from where we lived. I worked and worked that pretty summer afternoon to get the car spotless and just right to show my dad and make him proud. Right after I washed it and then dried the car ever so gently with a towel, I hopped in it to pull it around into the driveway. That was when I experienced a feeling I still have not forgotten to this day. Much to my surprise, I overlooked a stump that was right in front of where I washed the car, and I hit it with full force as I pulled forward. I got out and took one look at the front end of my dad's new car, and had one thought—*I am dead!*

My next move was to go and tell him what I had done. I was a nervous wreck. I had just torn to pieces the front end of the car and we still had to somehow drive it home in that condition. I will never forget that conversation with my dad. My lips were quivering. My palms were sweating. Tears were beginning to form in my eyes as I said the words, "Dad, you need to come look at your car." Having no idea how my dad would respond, I braced myself for the worst. He had never yelled at me in anger before, but this would be an opportune moment if ever there was one for him to cut loose and express his deep frustration and disappointment.

Surprisingly, he really did not say much at all. He did not yell. He did not even so much as say angry words. He never said a single negative thing to me about it. He knew it was an accident, and he could tell I was already feeling terrible for the mistake I made. We made it home that evening with part of the grill dragging the ground and noises that would make the screech of a cat whose tail had been stepped on sound bearable. We were soon able to laugh about the whole thing, and through that the understanding I already had of my dad loving me unconditionally was reinforced. It was through him and many incidents like this that I got a taste of God's perfect love for me even when I blew it. And it is this perfect love that can hold me in unbroken fellowship with Jesus.

> **The closer we are to God, the more we want to learn to honor the quality of our relationship with Him.**

As we grow closer to God, we begin to realize how much our relationship with Him means to us, and this motivates us to not want to do anything that will grieve Him or cause Him pain. I recall another incident that involved me and my dad. It was around the same time frame—in my early teen years. A female friend of mine and I wrote letters to each other all the time. We were very close friends and everything in our friendship was morally above board. I am not exactly sure what motivated me to do this, but one day I remember writing her a letter that included some very inappropriate language. I had never done that before. I did not even use inappropriate language in my daily conversations with people. For whatever reason, I thought using bad words in this instance would make me seem really cool to my female friend. I guess my conscience got to me after a while because I decided to not deliver the letter to her. Instead, I decided to get rid of it. I did not want the letter to be found by anyone, so I flushed it down the toilet. Or so I thought.

Returning home one day with my dad from a trip we had taken just a few days after the flushing of the letter, we pulled into the driveway. My dad turned the car off. Then he began explaining to me that he noticed the toilet in the back of the house was clogged and he had a tough time getting it unplugged. Then he said the words that caused my heart to fall through the floor: "I could not get the toilet unclogged, so as a last resort I reached with my hand to see if I could clear the object that stopped it up. When I did, I pulled out a wad of paper." Press pause for just a moment. Can you even begin to imagine what was going through my mind at that time? I was literally scared to death. Once again, I waited anxiously to see where my dad was heading with this story of the letter he had found in the toilet. May I say again how surprised I was by his response as he went on to explain how he opened up the letter and read it?

Amazingly, the toilet water did not destroy the letter or even cause any of the ink to run. Talk about getting caught red-handed! By God's grace, my dad handled yet another one of my blunders like a champion. He could have told me how disappointed he was in me for using such foul language in a letter, and to a girl no less. Instead, he said, "Son, I went through and circled some things you said in the letter that concerned me, and I want to encourage you to get alone with God and talk to Him about them. Ask Him to give you wisdom in this." Then he sent me on my way. Once again, I was given a taste of the goodness of God through the way my father responded to my failure. And once again, I realized how important my relationship with my dad really was and how I never wanted to grieve him in the same way ever again.

To this day, my dad and I are extremely close, and I would never want to say or do anything that would harm the quality of our relationship. The same goes in your relationship with God. The closer you are to God, the more you want to learn how to honor the quality of your relationship with Him. The goal is unbroken fellowship.

Through it all, God's promise remains—never will He leave you, never will He forsake you. His Spirit abides in every heart that has trusted in Him completely for being rescued from the death grip of sin and eternity apart from Him. The new heart He has placed within you comes with a new beginning, a new you. The process God is now walking you through is one of heart and life construction as He chips away at those areas of character that need reshaping. You are being made more and more into the character of God. As we continue our journey into the next and final chapter, realize it is one thing to be aware of God's plan for your life. It is another to see it in "The Power of a Clear Vision."

Making It Personal

- Were you aware of God's promise that He will never leave nor forsake you? What does that promise do for your faith?

- How does the idea of having a new heart and a new beginning from God strike you?

- What has been the most challenging for you when it comes to avoiding pitfalls?

- Who do you have to support you when you find yourself in the throes of personal failure?

Chapter 7

The Power of A Clear Vision

Chapter 7: The Power of a Clear Vision

"Then Jesus placed his hands on the man's eyes again, and
his eyes were opened. His sight was completely restored,
and he could see everything clearly" (Mark 8:25).

Many great books have been written on the subject of vision. Such books include vision for your company, church, sports organization, personal life, and so on. Vision has become the buzzword upon which great successes have hung their hat. Perhaps one of the main reasons why you have lived much of your life as a dancing chicken is because you have never established clear vision for your life. When you do not have clear vision, successes are rarely realized.

We have even come to associate certain leaders with great vision, and we often refer to them as *visionaries*. Visionaries (and in my opinion, any true leaders) have the ability to see a desired outcome and effectively lead, communicate, and inspire others toward that outcome. One such visionary of our time was Walt Disney. Here was a man who clearly had a vision for establishing a mini-sized perfect world, one filled with fun, laughter, and memories that would last a lifetime. Even though he died before his vision was brought to completion, he knew exactly what it was going to be like—simply because he was able to see it before anyone else.

Misunderstandings about Vision

I used to think vision was a type of mysterious knowledge that came down from the heavens and filled the minds of only a small select group of people—like Walt Disney—who were set apart to do great things. Then I began hearing people say how important it was to get a vision for my life personally, for my family, and for my vocation. This seemed like such a huge expectation, an almost impossible task. How could a common man like me actually come up with a legitimate vision, or better yet, how would I recognize it if I had one?

Nonetheless, I began setting out as a young man to get a vision for everything pertaining to my life. I read great books on vision. I researched countless vision statements developed by companies, churches, and individuals alike. I listened to great communicators talk about vision. I seemed to have gathered more information about vision than a person would need in order to create vision for their life. There was only one problem—nothing that I compiled in my research adequately fit who I was as a person. It was always someone else's vision or someone else's definition of what a vision was supposed to be.

The Vision Inside of You

Admittedly, vision can be somewhat elusive and mysterious. Yet, as I have grown older and hopefully somewhat wiser, I have discovered that vision is available to the common man. As I have looked over my shoulder into my past, I now realize that I had vision all along, just without realizing it. Deep inside of me have been bits and pieces of vision for my life, family, and vocation that have been developing as I have developed as a person. I did not realize that vision comes from what is inside you, as opposed to something you gather from other people's ideas of what vision is supposed to be like, although other people can help shape and broaden the vision that has been cultivating inside of you.

> I have discovered that vision is available to the common man.

Vision is simply an intrinsic pair of binoculars that you use regularly to see where you are going and the person you are becoming. Vision is a set of ideals of who you want to be and what you want to accomplish. Vision also coincides with your heart's deepest desires and longings. I have never had a vision for my life or family that I did not also have the desire for.

Vision is much more than living with a fantasy-land mentality, never really working to accomplish anything while always hoping for your ship to come in one day in the future. Instead, vision is birthed inside of your very being and is waiting to come out of you as you learn to listen to what your heart is telling you.

One of the greatest living examples of personalized vision was the multitalented athlete, Bo Jackson. Bo was an extremely gifted athlete who was not satisfied with only playing one professional sport. On the contrary, Bo's personal vision for his career included excelling in two professional sports back to back—baseball and football. His natural ability and physique allowed him to do both with greatness, with neither sport shorted in time or talent. This was, and still is, unthinkable by most professional athletes. Most are doing well to earn a playing spot in just one sport. Thanks to Bo, the world was blessed to see him light up the stage on the baseball diamond with home runs and on the football field with dynamic, breathtaking moves as a running back. Likewise, your vision must be just that—*your* vision. Anything else will be like the shoe that never fits, or it will be a case of shorting yourself and the world of being blessed by your unique gifting.

Chances are you also have been operating out of vision, or at least some bits and pieces of vision. For some, you just may not have all the pieces put together yet, or you may not have put specific words to the vision for your life before now. For others, this emphasis on vision is just a reminder of what you have already come to learn and experience.

Vision brings life, hope, and inspiration when it is clear and attainable.

We need a vision that will sustain us through the best of times and the worst of times. Vision brings life, hope, and inspiration. We are all a work in progress. There is never a finish line, short of death, that allows us to rest easily, never again having to worry about whether we will accomplish our vision and become all we want to become as individuals and families. It is a daily, moment by moment surge uphill, with two steps forward and sometimes multiple steps backward. Nevertheless, we need vision. Here are a few snapshots of what Shannon and I want our family's vision to look like in daily life. Again, we do not do these perfectly. It is a daily process of learning and growing and learning from failure. Before writing these, I sat down with my wife and kids and asked them to describe what we are about as a family. These are some of their responses:

- We tell each other several times daily that we love each other. We give a lot of hugs and kisses.

- To solve our problems, we will talk it out instead of yelling, screaming, or acting as though problems do not exist.

- As parents, we seek to demonstrate respect toward people in authority, and we expect our kids to follow suit. We will not tolerate disrespect or deliberate disobedience in the home or anywhere else from our kids.

- We focus on building relationships with our kids and limiting the number of rules we initiate.

- We seek to commit what we do as a family to prayer.

- We make it our aim to have ongoing conversations about what God is teaching us in the Bible. Many such conversations include decisions that need to be made, and we involve our kids in the decision-making process as much as is appropriate and possible.

- We laugh a lot and we have a lot of fun just being together.

> You should be able to clearly know when you are fulfilling your vision and when you are not.

In pursuit of having a home filled with these much-needed qualities, we have discovered five basic building blocks that play a critical role in supporting our family's vision. As I give these five building blocks to you, there are fundamental truths that I want to bring into clear focus that are essential in understanding vision. I have alluded to these in different ways throughout this chapter, but I think there is value in setting them apart.

First, vision is *personal*. You cannot just go out and adopt verbiage from someone else's vision and call it your own. It must come from within, from who you are as a person. It must be true to who you are as an individual and as a family.

Second, vision is *practical*. If your kids cannot explain it to you, it is too complicated. You should be able to clearly know when you are fulfilling it and when you are not.

Third, vision is *not self-sustaining*. It requires having the right building blocks in place serving as its foundation. You can have a vision to build the world's tallest building, but it is the ground floor that matters most and makes the rest possible.

There are at least five foundational building blocks that are allowing my family to realize our vision more and more as we keep our eyes on the prize. We did not sit down and decide one day that we will live our lives based on these five things. As you well know, life does not come to you neatly scripted in outline form. However, these building blocks have clearly surfaced as the main elements that have kept the vision for our family moving forward. Without these, our vision becomes shaky at best and could easily end up in the vision junkyard. With them, your vision can soar. Without them, your vision will have trouble making it off of the launch pad. And you will find yourself and your family hopping back on the stage, ready to yield to our culture's expectations.

Building Block #1: Absolute Trust

Trust is the baseline virtue to any lasting relationship. Trust is the one thing you cannot do without, and in many ways it is all you have. It takes a lifetime to build trust. It takes one bad decision to lose it. Once it is lost, it can take years to regain it, if at all.

> Trust is the baseline virtue to any lasting relationship.

Within the family, trust serves much like the immune system to the body. When it is strong, it takes a lot more than just the average cold to take you down. When it weakens even the slightest bit, almost anything can get the best of you. Because trust begins in the marriage relationship, it should be our first area of defense that we build in order to have the necessary trust level within our home that will enable us to fight off the many attacks that come our way—attacks that can destroy our most prized relationships.

Establish a "No Secrets" Policy

Establish a "no secrets" policy within your marriage. At first glance, this may seem like water under a bridge—a no-brainer for those who have tied the knot. It should have been part of the covenant you made at the altar the day you exchanged vows. Unfortunately, it is easier to begin keeping a log of secrets from your spouse than we would like to admit. Secret log-keeping can be done without giving it much thought. For many people, the log of secrets even begins before the wedding day.

Living with complete transparency in front of your spouse with no secrets to cover up allows you to live with each other in freedom and joy. You do not have to live in fear of them finding something out about you. Nor do you have to live in fear of finding out something about your spouse that they have chosen not to tell you somewhere along the way.

Since Adam and Eve's story in the garden of Eden, it has been second nature for humankind to hide when we have done something wrong. After Adam and Eve disobeyed God's command to not eat from the tree in the middle of the garden, we find them hiding from, of all people, God! We find their story in Genesis 3:8: "When the cool evening breezes were blowing, the man and his wife heard the LORD God walking about in the garden. So they hid from the LORD God among the trees." Men and women may not literally go and hide from their spouse like Adam and Eve hid from God, but they will hide money stashed in a drawer to support a habit their spouse knows nothing about. They will hide unannounced purchases and receipts. Some will hide addictions. Others will hide affairs.

> For many people, the log of secrets even begins before the wedding day.

For every decision you make to hide something from your spouse, you place an invisible wedge between you and them. For every wedge placed between you and your spouse, you lose closeness and intimacy, which are lifelines desperately needed in order for the marriage to survive. It then becomes a matter of time before all the cards in your deck of lies and secrecy come crashing down, leaving the relationship with little hope of making it.

The intimacy and closeness that you and your spouse experience in your marriage will be in direct proportion to the level of trust you share in the relationship. The greater the transparency is between the two of you, the deeper the trust. The more secrets you have, the shallower your intimacy will be until you choose to expose the secrets in all of their truth. So the answer to why you should expose your secrets to your spouse is that by doing so, it will give you the opportunity for your relationship to grow closer than ever before. It will empower you to live freer and love stronger than you could possibly imagine.

> The intimacy and closeness that you and your spouse experience in your marriage will be in direct proportion to the level of trust you share in the relationship.

Building Block #2: Respecting Authority

Sometimes a picture really is worth a thousand words. A recent cartoon on a social media site caught my attention. The cartoon was broken into two images, the first representing a time period of several decades ago, and the second representing our current society. In the first, a mom and dad were visiting their child's school teacher. While standing next to the teacher and holding up a copy of the child's report card, the parents shouted at their child, "What is the cause of these poor grades?"

The second image, representing modern day society, showed the same parents now standing beside the child and shouting the same words, except this time at the teacher. "What is the cause of these poor grades?" The message was clear—there has been an overwhelmingly obvious shift in the mindset of our culture that does not want to accept responsibility, and this includes parents when things do not turn out the way they hoped with their kids. In the cartoon, the parents in the second image demonstrated not only blame toward the teacher for the child's failing grades, but also communicated to their child that it is okay to be disrespectful to people in positional authority.

By using this example, I am not advocating that teachers cannot or do not sometimes make mistakes. They are human just like the rest of us. Nor am I suggesting that we should not defend our kids. There is an appropriate time and place for that. The reality I am addressing is that our culture has thrown respect for authority out the window and in its place has adopted a victim mentality, accompanied by an attitude of defiance.

Respect for authority begins inside the home with the examples set by Mom and Dad toward each other. Dad, if you have the habit of yelling at your wife or being demanding in your tone with her in front of your kids, you can expect your children (especially your sons) to eventually mirror your actions toward your wife in their tone and volume. They will also be prone to carry this mindset into their marriage relationship, thinking it is okay to treat their wife this way because Dad acted this way toward Mom while they were growing up. This has serious, long-term ramifications and should not be laughed off as irrational or minimal.

> Our culture has thrown respect for authority out the window and in its place has adopted a victim mentality accompanied by an attitude of defiance.

Mom, if you have the habit of undermining your husband's role of leadership in the home in front of your kids (especially your daughters), rest assured you are setting the stage for your daughters to ignore your husband's leadership and authority when they reach the teen years, the time when your husband's influence is needed the most in their lives. Your daughters will also likely undermine their future husband's role of authority in the home and continue to pass their attitude of disrespect on to the next generation.

Respect for authority begins with spouses showing proper respect at all times toward one another, especially when children are present. Respect continues by guarding what you say about people in authority behind closed doors. What you say in the privacy of your home about people in authority is not just your business—it can be just as influential to your children's perspective of authority as seeing you respond to authority in real life situations outside the home.

If you have the habit of criticizing your son's coach in the hearing of your son while perched on the couch in your living room, you are setting your son up to develop a defiant attitude toward his coach in the future, making him, not coincidentally, un-coachable. If you disagree with how the cheerleading coach seems to be leading the cheer squad your daughter is on, the worst thing you can do for your daughter is lower yourself to the level of the kids, jump on the bandwagon, and talk negatively about the coach with your daughter on the way home from the game. Instead, encourage your son or daughter to try to see things from their coach's perspective, and if necessary go privately to the coach and do your best to talk through things accordingly.

> Our kids need to see us model respect for authorities
> by guarding what we say about authorities behind
> closed doors and by how we respond or react in real life
> situations toward authority outside the home.

A couple of years ago I was pulled over two different times by two different policemen. I have been pulled over before and have had mostly pleasant experiences with policemen. These two times, however, were very different. The policemen (from two different counties) were very hateful, and each time my son was with me. I would never desire to argue with a policeman or intentionally show disrespect. I have to say, though, that I was less than pleased with the disrespect shown to me in these instances and I wanted to talk back. Yet there was an overriding thought going through my mind during those moments of deep frustration, which I am grateful for having as I look back on it now. I would set my son up to win or fail in the future with people in authority by how he saw me responding to the police. So, I kept my mouth shut and later explained to my son why.

Our kids need to see us acting respectfully toward each other. They need to see us model respect for authorities by guarding what we say about them behind closed doors and by how we respond or react in real life situations toward authority outside the home. We can bring respect for authority back to our society, but we will do it one child, one moment at a time. All future generations are depending on it. If you want peace in your home, make respect for authority (including your own as a parent) non-negotiable.

Building Block #3: Discipline for a Larger Purpose

Let me start off this section by saying if you are looking for surefire effective ways to discipline your kids that will guarantee they will turn out to be productive citizens in the world, you have bought the wrong book. As I said in the introduction of the book, I am a deeply flawed parent trying to find my own way through the maze of raising kids and hoping they will turn out right. Let us be honest about this—raising kids is a very messy and rewarding process. There are extreme ups and downs, heartaches and joys, wins and losses.

There is no possible way I can communicate dogmatically how you should be raising your children. At the same time, there are a few core needs children have that can guide us in the decision-making of how, when, and why we discipline them. Much of this is common sense stuff—things for which we could probably just use some helpful reminders. I know I need to be reminded regularly.

> Without proper discipline when they are young, you will literally create a monster that society will have to deal with for the rest of your child's life.

During the early years (roughly birth through age five or six) your child needs very clear boundaries set for them and very swift discipline when those boundaries are crossed. This helps establish in the child's mind an understanding that A plus B equals C during these formative years in their life when their personality is being developed. The goal is to help your child understand, "If I choose to do what my parents tell me not to, I am going to experience something rather unpleasant." You cannot reason with a four-year-old. They are too smart and will win most every time.

Believe it or not, your child can tell if you are a secure parent or an insecure parent by how you choose (or choose not) to discipline them. If you are an insecure parent, you will parent insecurely and inconsistently. It is the equivalent of having a substitute teacher in school, which I served as for a year. If you do not get your bluff in early, the students will run over you completely no matter their age. If you fear that you will push your child away by disciplining them, I can empathize with you to a certain point. However, if you are more concerned with keeping your child happy and making sure they like you than with shaping the direction of your child's life, then I must say this with a heart filled with compassion: without proper discipline in your child's life when they are young, you will literally create a monster whom society will have to deal with for the rest of your child's life. You are setting them up for failure and for a lifetime of very hard knocks that could be avoided. No one wants to be around an unruly kid. Be the parent! You can do this and you must.

Where I believe most parenting failures (including my own) occur, however, is when we seek to establish consistent discipline in the home, all the while forgetting that we are shaping a child's heart, not just their behavior. Your goal in discipline is not to kill your child's spirit or just curb their behavior for the moment but to shape their heart and character for a lifetime. For some of us, this shift in our thinking may be quite a challenge. It will require you to not only think differently about discipline but also to think beyond the moments of frustration to see the bigger goal.

Every child is different in how they respond to different types of discipline. You may have one child who cries when you just give them a certain parenting look. You may have another child who will not change their misbehavior if you spank them one time after another for doing the same disobedient thing. It all comes down to understanding your child's unique needs and heart.

> Your goal in discipline is not to kill your child's spirit or just to curb their behavior for the moment, but to shape their heart and character for a lifetime.

There is always a balancing act we, as parents, find ourselves in with our kids that is very normal and healthy. We all struggle at times with whether we are hitting the mark with how we discipline, whether we are acting too heavily or not enough. I believe the bottom line to all of it, however, is exactly what a friend of mine has said time and time again—it all comes down to whether we are disciplined enough ourselves as parents to stay in tune with the hearts of our kids and are willing to shape them through appropriate discipline even when it is difficult. It is truly about the heart—theirs *and* ours.

As your children move into young adolescent and teen years, they need you to have an increasingly stronger grip on who they are as individuals, on what makes them tick and what shuts them down. In simple terms, they need to have a growing relationship with you. While the idea of building a relationship with your child may cause you to fear losing your parental authority in their life, I want to make the case that the quality of your relationship with them will determine the effectiveness of the discipline you initiate. Instead of starting with the question of how to discipline your children as they grow older, consider starting with the question of how to grow a stronger relationship with your children so that your discipline (when needed) will be more effective.

Let us look at a contrast between two broad types of discipline. For our purposes, we will call them relationship-driven discipline and rules-driven discipline. Again, we will look at these primarily in the context of kids who are moving into the adolescent and teen years. Contrary to how it may appear, relationship-driven discipline is not referring to the relationship between your paddle and your child's backside. It does, however, have everything to do with your personal relationship with your children. Relationship-driven discipline seeks a balance between relationship-building and sticking to appropriate consequences when needed. This type of discipline is more concerned with staying connected to the heart of your child and trying to understand the *why* behind their negative behavior than it is with getting the paddle out due to the fact that another rule has been broken. Conversations become means of resolving disagreements and bringing understanding to one another's viewpoints rather than, say, an immediate loss of privileges with little or no conversation between parent and child.

> The quality of your relationship with your child will determine the effectiveness of the discipline you initiate.

Rules-driven discipline tends to place heavy emphasis on rule-making and rule-breaking. This approach is not nearly as concerned with the *why* behind a child's negative behavior, but is focused primarily on the visible deeds of the child. Many parents fear losing control of their kids as they get older, so their response is to increase the number of rules, hoping it will bring about the desired result of kids acting responsibly. Parents who operate within this type of framework of rules-driven discipline tend to relate to their kids much like a principal who upholds the student handbook at school.

Again, I want to bring back to the forefront the reality that all kids are different and some may need a stricter environment of clear dos and don'ts even into their late teen years. Some kids make it their mission in life to find the loopholes in every household rule; thus, stricter expectations in black and white may be needed. The point I want to make in the grand scheme of things is that you cannot increase the rules without increasing the relationship side of things with your kids and expect things to turn out right. As the saying goes, more rules for your kids without more relationship with you as the parents will only lead to more rebellion on the part of your kids.

As you can see, I want to affirm relationship-driven discipline as the norm, and I want to do so for a number of reasons. First and foremost, as a parent the emotional connection you have with your child is of utmost importance. Your child will respect you or be afraid of you depending on the kind of heart connection you have developed with them. For the record, they need a healthy dose of fear of your authority as the parent, but they do not need to go around being afraid of you. There is a big difference, and it all has to do with your heart connection with them. They will either feel safe to talk with you about the many important things going on in their life or they will hide them from you in fear of getting in trouble for being honest.

I am not advocating that you become your child's best friend in the sense of losing the God-given role of authority in the home. At the same time, there is a way to build loving trust with your kids that will encourage them to be open with you and want to be around you without feeling like they are walking on pins and needles. Your home is the primary place of preparing your children for life on their own. That does not mean, however, that you have to turn your home into a military boot camp. Your discipline can bring great results to prepare your child for whatever future God has planned for them. If you are content with just barking orders, however, it is a sure sign that you are either not willing or not capable of investing emotionally in your child. The unfortunate reality is that this will be reaped by your child later in life if there is not a significant change in you as the parent to recognize your child's need of being close to you and to your heart.

> You cannot increase the rules without increasing the relationship side of things with your kids and expect things to turn out right.

Having spent time in the previous chapter on connecting with your kids, let me just reiterate that one of the greatest ways I know to build relationships with your kids is to spend time having fun with them. Life cannot be all serious. Your household needs a lot of laughter and fun interaction together. If you are so busy being the professional at work and being the boss at home that you forget to be the life-bringer to the party, your kids will miss out on some of the greatest times of their life with you. This does not have to mean spending a lot of money on your kids. It means they would love it if you initiated a pillow fight with them when they least expected it. It means taking your child on in a competitive game and rubbing it in when you win. It means stealing a lick of ice cream from your child's cone when they look away. Bringing a playful atmosphere into your relationship with your kids is really what will pay big dividends in life later on. These things will not just happen. It must be an intentional part of your parenting, every bit as much as your discipline. What can you initiate today that involves having fun with your kids?

Another way to keep the relationship with your kids moving in the right direction is to find ways of bringing up touchy subjects in the context of having a good time together. Part of what makes discipline difficult is the fact that we normally only deal with problems in the heat of the moment when we have been made aware that a problem has occurred. In other words, we tend to be reactionary instead of proactive in finding out important information about our kids. Instead of waiting until you find a text between your child and a person you have asked them not to communicate with, take some time while baking cookies together and just ask a question to get the conversation going. For instance, you could ask your daughter, "Hon, how do you feel like you have done with staying away from so-and-so? Has that been a tough thing?" And wait for their response. If you get a favorable response from them, then maybe you can take the conversation a little further without pushing them over the edge of having to defend themselves. If you get an angry response, then back away and redirect the conversation to a safe topic that will bring the enjoyment back to baking cookies together.

> Your household needs a lot of laughter and fun interaction together as much as possible.

By intentionally and carefully finding ways to bring up the hard subjects in the context of safety and enjoyable moments, you will help build your relationship with your child, build deeper trust between the two of you, and hopefully eliminate a lot of knock-down drag-out fights later. Something inside of me just said that in the mind of the reader, I am talking mainly to the mom. Not so. This applies every bit as much to dads. No passing the buck here on the relationship building. In fact, Dad, you are the first and foremost person this applies to if you are in your child's life.

Second, also from the father's point of view, your children derive their deepest sense of identity and worth from you as a man. It is from you that they gain their deepest sense of security. If your child feels emotionally disconnected from you, they will try to fix that disconnection often times through misbehavior. They will act out in an effort to win back your attention even if it gets them into trouble. If you have a daughter, the older they get the more likely they will lean toward unhealthy dating relationships in an attempt to fill the void that they need you to fill as their father. It is for this reason that I am completely against a harsh, strictly authoritarian approach to parenting. Your children need to hear you tell them you love them. They need you to hold them when they are hurting and to hug them often. Your appropriate physical bond with your children is what creates the emotional bond they so desperately need with you.

I have to say this—your children are not just the fruit of your marriage relationship that you push to get out of your house as soon as possible so that you can go on with your all-important life. Your children are unique and beautiful creations of God who need your loving guidance and direction on how to make life work. They need your heart to be connected to theirs and (to mention it again) to know they are safe when they are around you. They must know they are deeply loved even if they mess up, that you want them around, and that you believe in them even when having to discipline them. This approach allows you to be firm without being cold and distant. When the relationship quotient is strong, the necessary rules tend to be few.

The goal of your discipline should be to not only strengthen your child's character but to maintain your heart connection with them. When your children feel close to you, they will want to do their best to please you with their decisions and choices. When they feel distant from you or if they feel as if the goal in life is to make sure they stay off your naughty list, they very well may try unimaginable things to try to get on your naughty list just to get your attention and try to regain closeness to you.

I do not know about you, but when I think about my kids being turned loose in this world, my radar goes up, my heart sinks, and I get a little worried about how they will make it in life on their own. The greatest way for me to prepare them for life is to do everything I can to keep a strong heart connection with them and protect them from as many adversaries as possible while they are under my care.

The most dangerous thing I can do is sever myself from them emotionally, leaving a dad-sized void for them to try to fill that lends itself to inappropriate relationships with people who do not care for their well-being. Will we as men ever do this perfectly for our children? No, but the more awareness we have of this, the better we can be equipped to fulfill our God-given role in the home.

If you grew up with a distant father, you may have a few more mountains to climb in order to get where you need to be with this whole heart connection thing with your own children. You know deep down, though, that they are worth every ounce of effort you invest into strengthening your relationships with them. Lest you doubt the importance of this, I will ask you a simple question: Were there not times in your growing up years when you wished your dad would have not only been there, but would have taken the time to say I love you? To put his arm around you and let you know he believed in you and that it was going to be okay? To listen, not just to your words but to your heart? To care about your needs behind your deeds instead of just breaking the paddle out any time you broke a rule or made a mistake? I rest my case.

Your kids do not need you any less than you needed the closeness of your own parents. If your kids are still in your home, or even still in your life at all, the great thing is that it is not too late to make progress in developing a heart connection with them that can last the rest of your life and theirs. Laugh a lot together. Bring the fun to the party. Initiate conversations on touchy subjects in the context of fun times together, and give your relationship with your kids a chance to continue growing.

A Unified Front

Nothing we have talked about so far regarding discipline will be of any value until you and your spouse are on the same page when it comes to discipline. I am not suggesting that you cannot share different opinions in your parenting styles, but you must be of one accord in your plans of action or your kids will create a wedge between you wide enough for a tractor trailer to drive through. Part of the struggle on how to discipline your kids comes from the simple fact that you and your spouse grew up in different households with different expectations. In ideal situations, spouses will have talked through at least some of this prior to marriage or prior to bringing kids into the world. More often than not, though, it is a work in progress and we are all working hard to get our bearings with how to effectively discipline our kids.

How to Get on the Same Page

For a starting point, one of the best things you can do to get on the same page with your spouse in the area of discipline is for each of you to get alone in a quiet place and write down the behavioral expectations you feel are most important for your kids. For instance, is it important for your kids to clean their room each night before going to bed? Should your kids have cell phones or portable media players, and if so what should be the shutoff time for those at night? Make a list of which are most important to you, then come together and share your lists. Discuss what you both agree and on what you disagree. As you work through the list, come up with how you want to approach disciplining your kids when they do not meet those expectations. If you and your spouse end up having a rough time coming to agreements, consider bringing in a trusted friend or counselor to help you work through the kinks. I would advise against it being another family member, however.

What you cannot afford to do is to allow the kids to work the two of you against each other in how you want to discipline them. One way to head this off is for you to talk with your spouse about how you wish to handle situations before reacting to them without your spouse's knowledge. It is the conviction of my home that I as the father will have the final say in how we carry out the discipline for our kids. My decision, however, is rarely made without the insight and perspective of my wife. This helps me make sure I am seeing situations from the right perspective and not just out of anger or frustration from what I perceive is true.

Who Should Carry Out the Discipline?

Obviously, if you are a single parent, you will have to be the initiator of discipline, though I would also empower grandparents and extended family as needed to help you in the process. If you are a step-parent, the discipline should be left up to the biological parent, but with your full support.

While some families may believe strongly that one spouse or the other should do most, if not all, of the discipline of biological children, my wife and I agree that the circumstances are what dictates which one of us carries out the discipline in our home. Without hesitation, though, it is clear that I serve as the heavy in our home for discipline.

My wife knows she has complete authority to get our kids in line over the day-to-day issues that stick their head up (e.g., the kids are arguing over who washed the dishes last and both are refusing to do them). As I mentioned earlier, Shannon is a very strong woman with a lot of discernment and has no problem holding her own when it comes to disciplining our kids. She also knows that at any time she can defer to me when needed. As a matter of fact, while writing this very section, I just received a text from my wife letting me know of an issue that has come up at school today with one of our children. There are times when my presence is needed as much as my words.

However you choose to go about this, at the end of the day you and your spouse must do whatever it takes to stay on the same page, so that your efforts in disciplining your kids will have the chance to have their full effect. Discipline with a larger purpose, one that sees beyond the moment and realizes the lifetime result of what you want your discipline to accomplish.

Building Block #4: Commitment

It seems that our culture is rapidly raising a generation of people who are committed to only one thing—remaining uncommitted to anything. How can we blame them? They have been raised in a society that promotes self-contentment at whatever cost, with no thought of anyone else, with little or no desire to give anything back. We have become a society characterized by a sense of entitlement. We have a generation that thinks it is entitled to happiness, wealth, positional status, and favor without having to lift a finger to earn any of it.

When it comes to commitment within a marriage, the wedding vows have become nothing more than a list of great sounding statements of how a couple intend to support each other. In reality, many couples would be much more in line with the truth if they came to the altar and said, "I am willing to give my fifty percent if my spouse gives their fifty percent to our marriage. As long as he changes and becomes who I want him to be and meets all my expectations…as long as she does not turn out to be like her mother…and as long as no one better comes along in a few years, then we should be okay."

Needless to say, what I am describing is a far cry from true commitment. When I speak of commitment, I am referring to an attitude, first within the marriage, that says in essence, "We are in this together— no matter what." If we have so much money that we never have to worry about paying our bills, or if we end up living paycheck to paycheck and having to go without some of life's finer amenities, we are staying together—no matter what. If we keep our youthful figure for decades or if things start going south all too quickly, we are together in this—no matter what. When you meet my expectations and when you go through seasons when you lose the capacity to meet my needs the way you once did, we will walk through it together—no matter what. When all we have is love for each other and a lifelong promise to stick it out for better or worse, we will finish this race called life together—no matter what.

> The first step of demonstrating true commitment to your spouse and kids is to remove all other options from your mind that would keep you from fulfilling your lifelong commitment to them.

The first step of demonstrating true commitment to your spouse and kids is to remove all other options from your mind that would keep you from fulfilling your lifelong commitment to them. A couple may fight for months and even years within the marriage and still survive. It seems, however, that when a viable option enters the picture that could serve as an "out" for one or both spouses, the marriage reaches an abrupt end. The options I am referring to could include another man or woman entering the picture, or a spouse's over-involved parents who pressure their son or daughter to move back home until things "settle down." Another very prominent option for many spouses is receiving a high-paying salary or job offer that would keep them from having to depend on their spouse financially. Whatever the option may be, if you desire to demonstrate true commitment to your family, kick the option out of your mind, do not even allow the word *divorce* to enter your vocabulary, and enjoy the fruits of a lifelong, committed relationship with your spouse.

Commitment also has a sacrificial ring to it. Commitment to marriage and family does not provide a seat on the bus for fair weather fans. You simply will not survive. If there is anything we as human beings do not do so well, it is making voluntary sacrifices for the benefit of others. The word *sacrifice* entails a trace of pain involved for the person doing the sacrificing. If you claim to be sacrificing a lot for your family but there is no pain involved for you personally, you are not sacrificing. You are only a professional complainer.

One of the struggles that baseball coaches have to deal with occasionally is asking a good batter at the plate to offer a sacrifice bunt in order to move a runner from one base to another. A bunt, for those of you not inclined to watch baseball, is when a batter squares around facing the pitcher, and tries to allow the pitched ball to barely hit their bat, allowing the ball to only go a few feet. The trade-off for getting runners moved to the next base is that you as the batter are willingly giving yourself up as an out for the good of the team. Personally, I would rather hit home runs than be asked to lay down a bunt and give myself up. I think we all would.

The greatest example of all time of personal sacrifice was found in Jesus Christ. It says in 1 John 3:16, "We know what real love is because Jesus gave up his life for us." The principle, however, does not end there. The passage of Scripture continues, "So we also ought to give up our lives for our brothers and sisters." What does sacrifice look like in the context of a home and family? It means giving up personal time, space, agendas for the benefit of others in your household. It may include something as simple as not always having control of the remote for the TV. It may include something much more costly, like taking on a second or third job in order to make ends meet. Without sacrifice on the part of everyone, commitment will be shallow and the enjoyments of family life short-lived.

> **The greatest example of all time of personal sacrifice was found in Jesus Christ.**

Once again, I must come back to the role of the husband and father as we talk about sacrifice. In just a few days, we will celebrate what is known as Father's Day. This is the one day out of the entire year when it is culturally admirable to esteem the millions of dads out there who are giving their best for the benefit of their family and the world. The giving of gifts—such as new grills, dress ties, new tools, fishing gear, and expressive cards—is what typically fills the schedule for the day.

I believe, however, as one speaking with hopefully some level of subjectivity, that we do an overall terrible job of honoring husbands and fathers on any other given day. The same is true of honoring mothers. There is, though, a higher requirement found in Scripture placed upon men that, when carried out by a man, deserves much more honor and respect than what is typically on our radar. It is found in Ephesians 5:25: "For husbands, this means love your wives, just as Christ loved the church. He gave up his life for her." This verse clearly explains the kind of love with which we are to love our wives, but it does not end there.

As husbands and fathers, we are to set the example of sacrifice for our families in how we live. We are called to shoulder more weight and responsibility than anyone else in the home. We are called to provide for our families and to keep the vision for our home moving forward. In its bare truth, at the heart of our vision we are called to die on behalf of our family. Not a literal death, though that sometimes may be necessary. More so, however, it is a death to self. Everyone benefits from a selfless husband and father. Everyone suffers from one who is absorbed in his own world and selfish desires.

> **Commitment is an attitude that says, "No matter what, we are in this together."**

This is why, I believe, men who live out their God-given calling of giving themselves up on behalf of their families are much more worthy of honor. From death comes life. This is true of seeds that are planted in the ground. It is also true of a man who dies to himself daily. His family receives the fruit that is born including blessing, honor, and life.

Commitment is an attitude that says no matter what, we are in this together. It requires you to do away with anything that could pose as an option, an "out" for you to consider taking that would remove you from your responsibilities to your spouse and family. Commitment means sacrifice. The more we give up on behalf of each other, the more we will enjoy the lasting fruit of joy, peace, and contentment within our homes.

Building Block #5: Effective Communication and Conflict Resolution

Communication is what makes the world go around. It is also one of the most common causes of conflict within a marriage and family. You are constantly communicating something—verbally or nonverbally—whether you realize it or not. Most of our communication is nonverbal, including posture, eye contact, facial expressions, even silence itself. It is a basic fact when it comes to verbal communication that women use several thousand more words than men do in a day. For some men, if you are able to get the slightest grunt out of them it would be considered progress. This is one reason why men will do anything they can to avoid getting into an argument with a woman. He knows she will slay him with her use of words. The result? Men try all the more to stay away from meaningful conversations, which in turn makes women angrier and they use even more words to get men to engage in conversation. When he finally does, it is normally not very pretty because it is fueled with built-up frustration. It is really a humorous dynamic when you stand back and think about it.

How do we reconcile these communication differences in a way that does not expect a man to mirror the communication skills of a woman nor a woman to communicate like a man? How do you take a relationship to a place where you feel heard and understood? Finally, how do you attempt to resolve conflicts without constantly trying to change the other person? These are all good questions that we will attempt to answer with clarity.

Let us begin by looking at the many factors that influence our communication, or lack of it, with each other, beginning with your home of origin. Chances are high that during your growing up years at home you adopted a way of communicating by watching your parents communicate, for good or for bad, and it has shaped a lot of how you now relate to others as an adult. The saying that opposites attract is never truer than how couples communicate with each other, including your parents. Typically one parent is the outgoing one, the life of the party, and never lacks something to talk about. The other parent is typically the laid back one, easy going, and takes life as it comes to them. They are also much less verbal. This communication dynamic seems great during the dating period as a couple is getting to know each other. In fact, these traits are likely to be the very things that attracted them to one other in the first place. She is everything he is not. He is everything she is not. A perfect match made in heaven. Eventually, however, their communication styles or habits can become their greatest weaknesses if they do not learn to make changes along the way. No matter your communication strengths or weaknesses, I want to provide several communication principles taken straight out of what I believe is the greatest relationships book in the world—the Bible. These can assist you in becoming a better communicator with your spouse and your children.

Listen more and talk less

James 1:19 says, "Understand this, my dear brothers and sisters: You must all be quick to listen, slow to speak, and slow to get angry." You have heard it said before that the reason God gave us two ears and one mouth was so we would listen twice as much as we speak. There are a few things we can do to help us become better listeners. They include:

- Make good eye contact with the person who is speaking.

- Listen with your heart as well as your ears.

- Provide positive nonverbal feedback to show that you are in tune with what the person is saying, such as nodding your head.

- Practice active listening. That is, once the person is finished speaking, attempt to repeat back to them what you heard them say, making sure you are on the same page with them.

- Avoid interrupting. Proverbs 18:13 reminds us that, "Spouting off before listening to the facts is both shameful and foolish."

Take a salt shaker with you wherever you go

Colossians 4:6 says, "Let your conversation be gracious and attractive so that you will have the right response for everyone." We all know that salt enhances flavor. Salt also purifies. When mixed with a lot of grace, it makes for some God-honoring conversations. Ephesians 4:15 gives us a better idea of what our conversations can and should look like when they are full of grace and seasoned with salt. It says,

"Instead, we will speak the truth in love, growing in every way more and more like Christ."

> We cannot afford to go through life with the attitude of just "telling it like it is." Our spouse and children deserve so much more from us than that.

Many people are professionals at speaking the truth. I do not know how many times I have heard someone say, "Well, I just tell it like it is!" The only problem with "just telling it like it is" is that it can demonstrate a lack of care, respect, and concern for the other person. In addition, if you are a follower of Christ, this type of attitude also neglects the next two words of the verse—*in love*. To speak the truth means setting aside any pretense and expressing what is really on your mind or in your heart. To speak the truth *in love* means that you recognize your words can, according to Proverbs 18:21, "bring death or life." I have heard it said that if we could see the wounds people carry on the inside the same way we can see the wounds they carry on the outside, we would treat each other much differently. Some of you reading this book right now can effortlessly recall words that have been spoken to you in the past that left significant scars on your soul. Words from parents, a coach, a friend, a coworker. Some of you may still be trying to recover from those hurtful words that cut you so deeply like a knife.

The problem with words is that once they leave your mouth, they can never be taken back. As adults, we are living out the results of the choices we have made through the course of our lifetime. I believe we are also living out the results of how we have handled what others have said to us along the way, both positively and negatively. We should permanently flush down the toilet the nursery rhyme that says sticks and stones may break our bones, but words can never hurt us.

When I was younger and playing for a baseball team, I recall vividly the many times I heard our coach scream profanity at his players. Thankfully he never let loose on me, but I can tell you without hesitation that his angry words had a significant impact on my life. I did not grow up in a household filled with yelling and profanity. So when I was exposed to this type of behavior from the coach, I did not cope well. I internalized a lot of anger over time from his hateful words spoken to my fellow players. It affected my health. I ended up losing over twenty pounds, and my performance was greatly hindered as a result.

Looking back, I recognize that much of why his negative attitude and harsh words affected me so much was simply due to my own emotional immaturity. However, I learned a rather painful lesson about the power of words and it has stuck with me ever since. We cannot afford to go through life with the attitude of just "telling it like it is." Our spouse and children deserve so much more from us than that. We need to show them the respect they deserve. Our words can bring healing and life or lifelong damage and even death to a soul.

Ditch the fish

Ephesians 4:29 says, "Don't use foul or abusive language. Let everything you say be good and helpful, so that your words will be an encouragement to those who hear them." How much differently do you think the world would be if we all chose to live by this simple verse in our everyday lives? About a year ago my family began to notice an unpleasant odor in my son's bedroom. We searched high and low, trying to identify the location of the spoiled glass of milk, the food left on a plate, or the shoes in the closet that soured after being played with outside in the rain. Much to our surprise, it was none of those things. My son just happened to be preparing for a trip when he pulled a backpack out of his closet. What unfolded next was something none of us could have ever expected in a million years. As my son unzipped his backpack, he pulled out a gallon baggie that contained what appeared to be the remains of a fish. A literal fish. My son had gone fishing however many weeks prior to this, caught a fish, and decided to bring it home with him to show us. The only problem was that he forgot about it. By this time, the fish had exploded in the baggie. The source of the stench had finally been uncovered.

> There is not a "do better" filter that can adequately help us control our tongues.

The word *foul* is a word that describes words spoken that literally sour the airwaves. They can be compared to someone carrying around a dead fish in their pocket for days on end. I have heard similar stories of men catching fish and putting them in the garage with the best intentions of cleaning them after dinner. One thing leads to another, the fish end up being forgotten about, and a few days later the whole house smells like death. What we need to take from this illustration is the fact that our unwholesome words have the same effect on our homes and on our relationships. If we are all in need of some improvement in this, we must ask the obvious question: How do we change this? How can we make improvements in our conversations with people, especially with those we love and care about the most?

Part of the reason why this particular area of our lives can be challenging for us to improve is the fact that we are all too used to going around with smelly fish in our pocket from using unwholesome words all the time. Now, being the nice people that we are, we will try to reason with ourselves and start to think that what we need to help us change this damaging characteristic is a "do better" filter. We will try to convince ourselves that a "do better" filter will be the antidote for the day that will help us clean up the air and empower us to begin using our words for the benefit of others, as the verse in Ephesians says.

There is only one problem—there is not a "do better" filter that can adequately help us control our tongues. James 3:8 says "No one can tame the tongue. It is restless and evil, full of deadly poison." Committing to "do better" with what comes out of our mouths would be the equivalent of putting a new fuel filter in your vehicle while failing to recognize that the gas tank is actually full of dirt and is the real source of the problem. After one or two cranks of the engine, the filter will only be clotted with dirt again, leaving the vehicle unusable.

Using this illustration, we need to first recognize that what comes out of our mouths is really just an overflow of what is in our hearts. Listen to Luke 6:45: "A good person produces good things from the treasury of a good heart, and an evil person produces evil things from the treasury of an evil heart. What you say flows from what is in your heart." You cannot expect lasting change to come in your conversations without having an ongoing change of heart.

This passage of Scripture in Luke paints a picture of two very different kinds of people—a good man and an evil man. I find it interesting that Luke goes to an extreme telling us that the way to tell a good man from an evil man is by listening to what comes out of his mouth. Jesus reiterated this very teaching in Matthew 15:17-19; Jesus told his closest followers, "Anything you eat passes through the stomach and then goes into the sewer. But the words you speak come from the heart—that's what defiles you. For from the heart come evil thoughts, murder, adultery, all sexual immorality, theft, lying, and slander."

You may be saying, "Well, I have been a Christian for twenty years and I am a good person." That is great, but do your conversations reflect that? I have been around people for months, even years at a time, never knowing they professed to be a follower of Jesus simply because of what came out of their mouth on a regular basis. To take that thought a little further, the word *produces* in Luke 6:45 in the original language means the continual bringing forth of something, not just a one-time occurrence. This verse does not mean, then, that a good person cannot have a bad day, a bad moment, or a slip of the tongue. It implies that what is coming from your mouth on a regular basis is the means for others to tell if you are a true follower of Jesus.

> What comes out of our mouths is really just an overflow of what is in our hearts.

The flip side of this is that it is impossible to expect good things to regularly come from the overflow of a heart that is full of evil. There absolutely must be a heart change that allows a person to be moved from the category of being "evil" to the category of being "good." This heart change is actually a heart exchange performed by God Himself, as we learned in chapter four. When that type of heart exchange occurs, one can rightly expect that the fruit of his mouth will become good-tasting fruit for everyone around—if they are diligent to store up the right things within them.

A good person, according to the text, is someone who is intentional to store up good things within their heart. The storing up process cannot be understated. It should be understood as a continual stashing away of resources that are used on a regular basis. It is the picture of someone at a grocery store, stocking the shelves with quality products that are in high demand by consumers. If you are a good person—that is, one who is in right standing with God—and are striving to live according to His commands, you cannot afford to hope that the good you stored within your heart last week will be enough to meet the demands for this week. Just like bread will eventually go stale if left on the shelf too long, so also your heart can become hardened, insensitive, and lacking spiritual nutrition if you neglect to fill it continually with good things. When this happens, you will begin to default back to your old way of doing things, and the good fruit will be missing from your life and from your conversation.

Clearing the Shelves

How does a person make sure they are storing up good things within their heart? First, you may need to make room for good things by ridding your heart of bad things that you have allowed on the shelf. For the Christ follower, this removal process is accomplished through two words you have probably heard before—confession and repentance.

To confess something that is impure and has been sitting on the shelf of your heart means more than just acknowledging that there is something inappropriate there that should not be. It means you must go into the darkest places within your heart, take hold of whatever is there that does not belong, and drag it out into the open with it kicking and screaming. Then you place it before God in prayer, agreeing with God that those things have been in your life, and with His help and grace, you are ridding your shelves of that which is harmful to your life. This is true confession.

> To confess something to God means you must go into the darkest places within your heart, take hold of whatever is there that does not belong, and drag it out into the open with it kicking and screaming.

Once you have removed the harmful things from the shelves of your heart, it is then necessary to immediately begin filling your heart with good stuff while at the same time being ever so aware of the impure things that are always trying to find a way back onto your shelves. There are a few basic ways of keeping the shelves stocked with good things, including reading the Bible daily. The Bible is God's visible spiritual nourishment for your life. In Matthew 4:4, Jesus said, "People do not live by bread alone, but by every word that comes from the mouth of God." With this in mind, we need a good starting point of what to read in the Bible. If you do not already have a daily reading plan, I encourage you to begin by reading a chapter in the book of Proverbs every day. There are thirty-one chapters in the book, which makes for a new chapter each day of the month. The quantity of what you read is not the important thing. The quality of what you read, digest, and store within your heart each day is what really matters.

In addition to reading the Bible, praying is essential to your ongoing goal of storing up good things within your heart. By praying, you can ask God to fill you with wisdom, knowledge, and understanding. He promises to provide these things for you upon your asking.

Another way to store up good within your heart is to surround yourself with people who are like-minded with you on things pertaining to God. God will use people who are walking with Him to speak things of excellent nutritional value into your life throughout your spiritual journey. Remember, words have the power of life!

Keep the Sword in the Sheath

The final principle for reshaping your conversations is to *keep the sword in the sheath*. Proverbs 12:18 says, "Some people make cutting remarks, but the words of the wise bring healing." To keep the sword in the sheath simply means you are willing to think before you speak. How much damage has been done by me—and perhaps by you—by what we have absentmindedly said in the presence of others? There is no such thing as a meaningless conversation or comment. We need to be aware of our conversation and put a guard over our mouths so that we can be life-givers instead of life-takers by what we say.

> There is no such thing as a meaningless conversation or comment.

Every family needs a clear vision of where you want to go and who you want to become. These five building blocks can assist in helping you get where you want to go as you weave them into your daily routine of family relationships. With them, you have a great chance of succeeding. Without them, your vision will likely be short-lived.

Making It Personal

- What is your family's vision? Take time to call a family meeting and discuss this in detail. Who do you want to be? Where are you going? What do you want your family to look like in five years?

- In which of the five building blocks do you believe your family is strong?

- In which of the five building blocks could you use improvement?

A Closing Word from the Author

I hope by reading this book that you have a renewed desire to break free from the unhealthy cultural expectations that have influenced your thinking and have kept your closest relationships from being all they were meant to be. While there is so much more that could and should be said, my hope is that you can take the basic structure—the overall game plan provided in this book—and pursue a vision for yourself and your family that will take you where you want to go.

You can do this. Life is just too short to live any other way. As a way to help you in the process, I invite you to visit my blog at http://baseballpreacher.wordpress.com. It is here that I have ongoing posts regarding much of the content found in this book, including blogs on faith, marriage, and family. I wish you the very best as you set out to break free from the unhealthy cultural expectations that have kept you living life like a dancing chicken!

About the Author

Phillip Taylor has more than fifteen years of local church ministry experience with a focus on teenagers and their families. Having served in the mental health field and in the public schools as a teacher and coach, he has seen firsthand how today's cultural pressures and expectations are negatively affecting family closeness and relational health. It is from this viewpoint that he writes this book, in addition to his shared experiences of raising a family of his own and enjoying twenty years of marriage with his wife, Shannon.

Phillip received his bachelor of science in education from Henderson State University and his masters in Christian education from Mid-America Baptist Theological Seminary. Phillip, Shannon, and their two teenage children live in the Ozark Mountains of northern Arkansas where they enjoy hunting, fishing, and sharing valuable time together.

Phillip can be contacted at: iamphilliptaylor@gmail.com.

More Titles by 5 Fold Media

1 Samuel
King's Commentaries
by Ryan King
$15.95
ISBN: 978-1-936578-4075-7

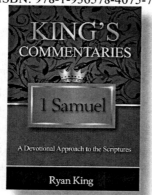

1 Samuel is a firsthand account of the riveting story of Israel's early monarchy. It follows the tumultuous struggle for relevancy of their most famous king, David. His remarkable story and the changes God brought into his life are the stuff of legend. But here they become understandable and applicable to our daily lives. Pastor Ryan, through a simple and easy-to-read style, opens up the pages of this book of the Bible with humour and grace; his stories and challenges will stay with you throughout the day.

Against Starlight
Discovering God
by Hermie Reynolds
$14.95
ISBN: 978-1-936578-73-3

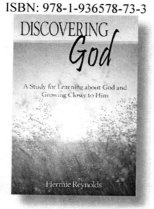

We live in a time where we see natural disasters like never before. These things cause us to ask questions.

Reading this book will bring greater understanding about the way God works. It is designed to be used individually or in small groups. Each chapter has discussion questions which will help you dig deeper into the Scriptures and apply what you learned to your life and situation.

"To Establish and Reveal"
For more information visit:
www.5foldmedia.com

Use your mobile device to scan
the tag and visit our website.
Get the free app:
http://gettag.mobi

Like 5 Fold Media on Facebook, follow us on Twitter!

CPSIA information can be obtained
at www.ICGtesting.com
Printed in the USA
FFOW01n0918280814
7075FF